KB270460

점프 업 파닉스 Jump Up Phonics

Phonics 1

개정판

점프 업 파닉스 1 [개정판]

2008년 05월 20일 초판 1쇄 발행
2025년 04월 15일 개정 1쇄 발행

지은이 문호준/국제어학연구소 영어학부
그림 이경택
펴낸이 이규인
펴낸곳 국제어학연구소 출판부
출판등록 2010년 1월 18일 제302-2010-000006호
주소 서울특별시 마포구 대흥로4길 49, 1층(용강동 월명빌딩)
Tel (02) 704-0900 **팩시밀리** (02) 703-5117
홈페이지 www.bookcamp.co.kr
e-mail changbook1@hanmail.net
ISBN 979-11-9880102-9 13740
정가 18,000원

· 이 책의 저작권은 〈국제어학연구소 출판부〉에 있습니다.
  저작권법에 의해 보호를 받는 저작물이므로 무단 전재와 복제를 금합니다.
· 잘못 만들어진 책은 〈국제어학연구소 출판부〉에서 바꾸어 드립니다.

Jump Up Phonics 1

개정판

글 문호준·국제어학연구소 영어학부

국제어학연구소

CONTENTS

Dd
Cc
Bb
Aa
Mm
Nn
Oo
Pp
Qq
Rr
Ss
9

Ee

Ff

Gg

Hh

Ii

Ll

Kk

Jj

Tt

Uu

Vv

Ww

Zz

Yy

Xx

Unit 1 Alphabet Aa Bb Cc

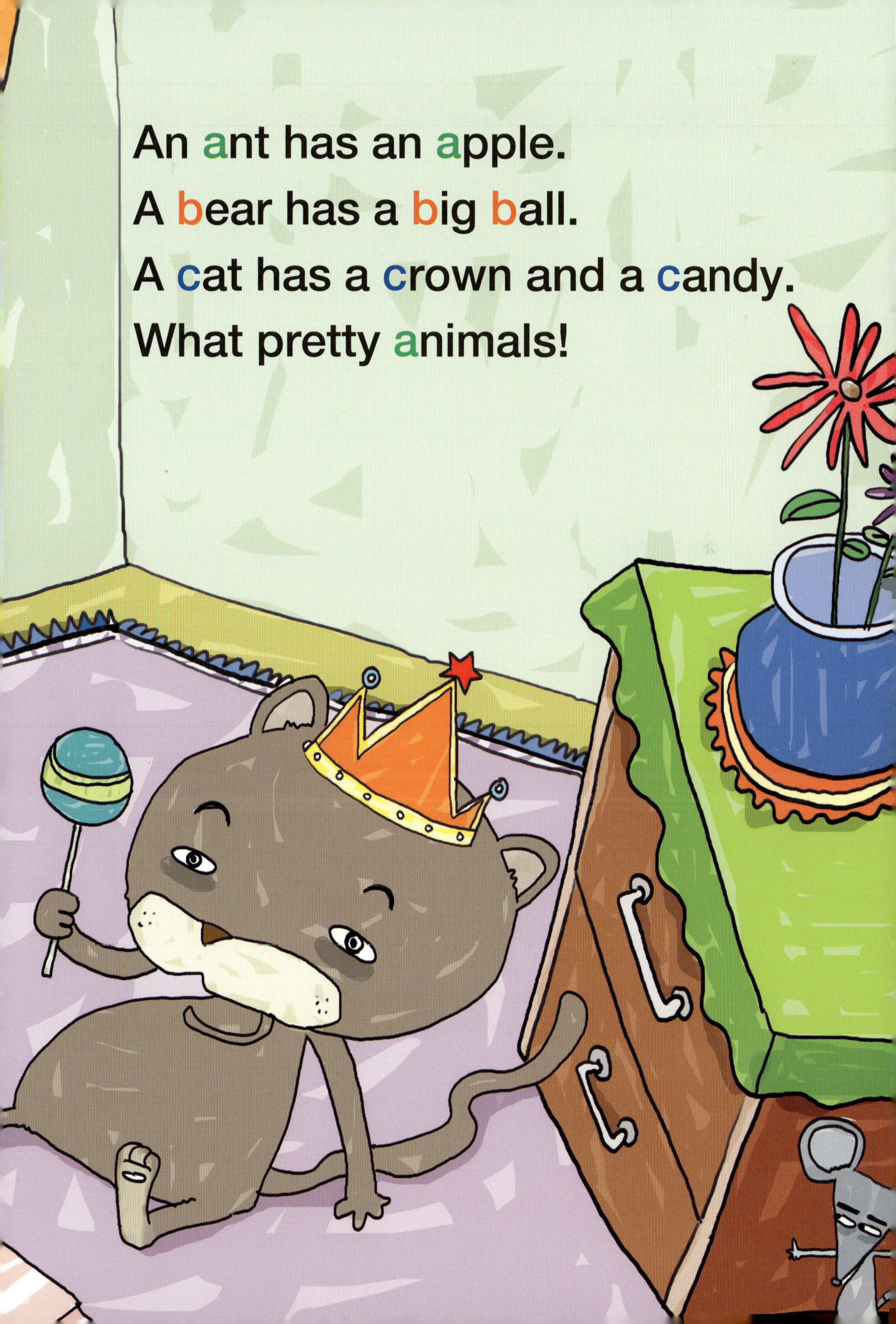

An ant has an apple.
A bear has a big ball.
A cat has a crown and a candy.
What pretty animals!

Listen and repeat.

A a

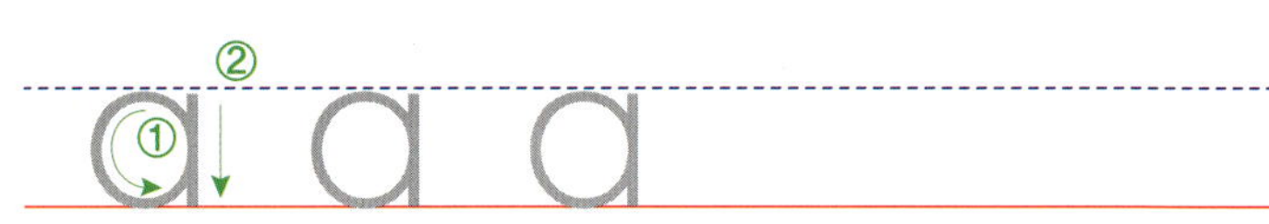

B b

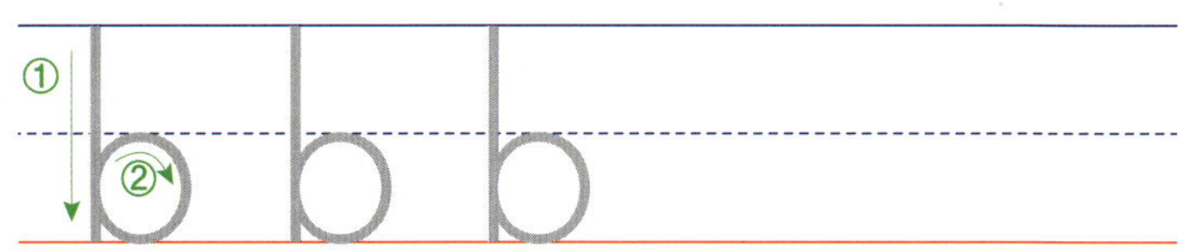

C c

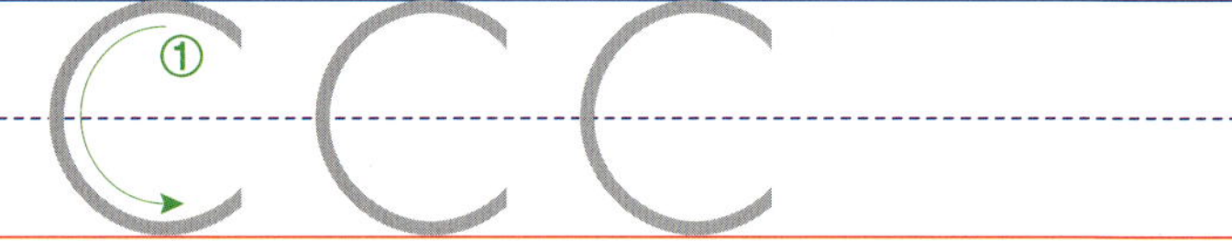

Listen, point and repeat.

ant

apple

animal

bear

big

ball

cat

crown

candy

Listen and check the beginning sound letter.

1

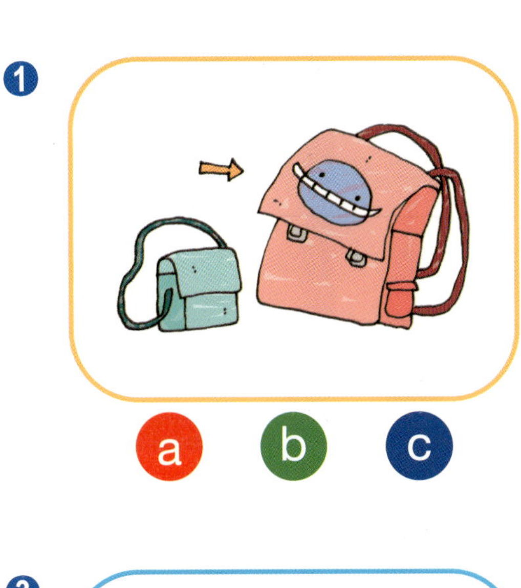

a　b　c

2

a　b　c

3

a　b　c

4

a　b　c

5

a　b　c

6

a　b　c

Color the same sound with the same color.

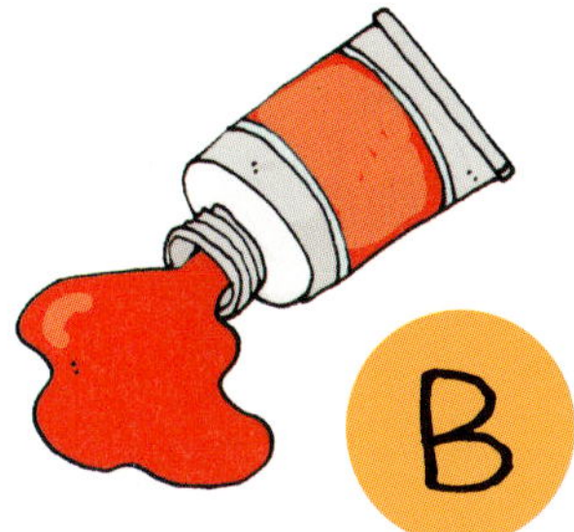

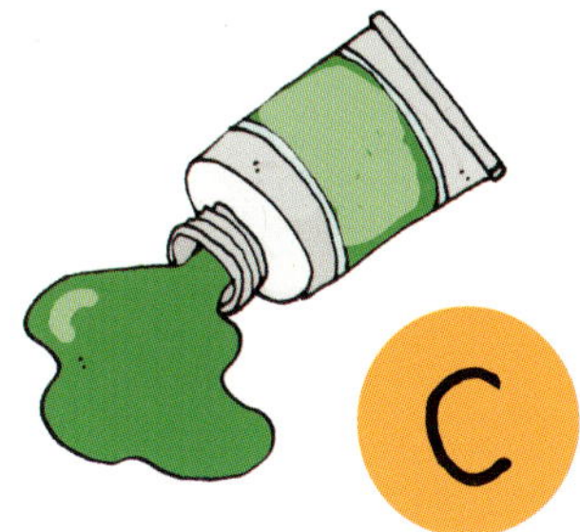

Circle the correct picture.

1 A a   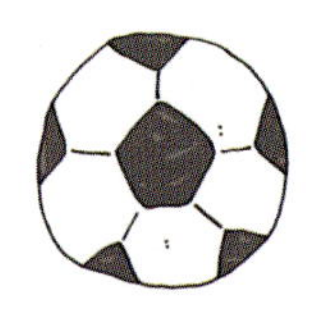

2 C c 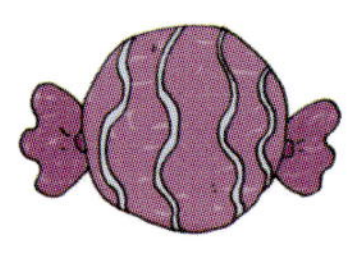  

3 B b  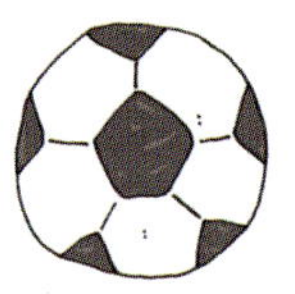 

4 B b  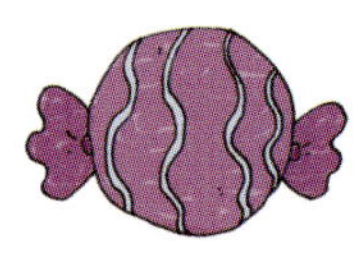 

5 C c   

Circle and write the missing letter.

1

a
b
c

__ a l l

2

a
b
c

__ p p l e

3

a
b
c

__ a n d y

4

a
b
c

__ a t

5

a
b
c

__ n t

6

a
b
c

__ e a r

Complete the crossword puzzle.

① 

② 

③ 

④ 

⑤ 

⑥ 

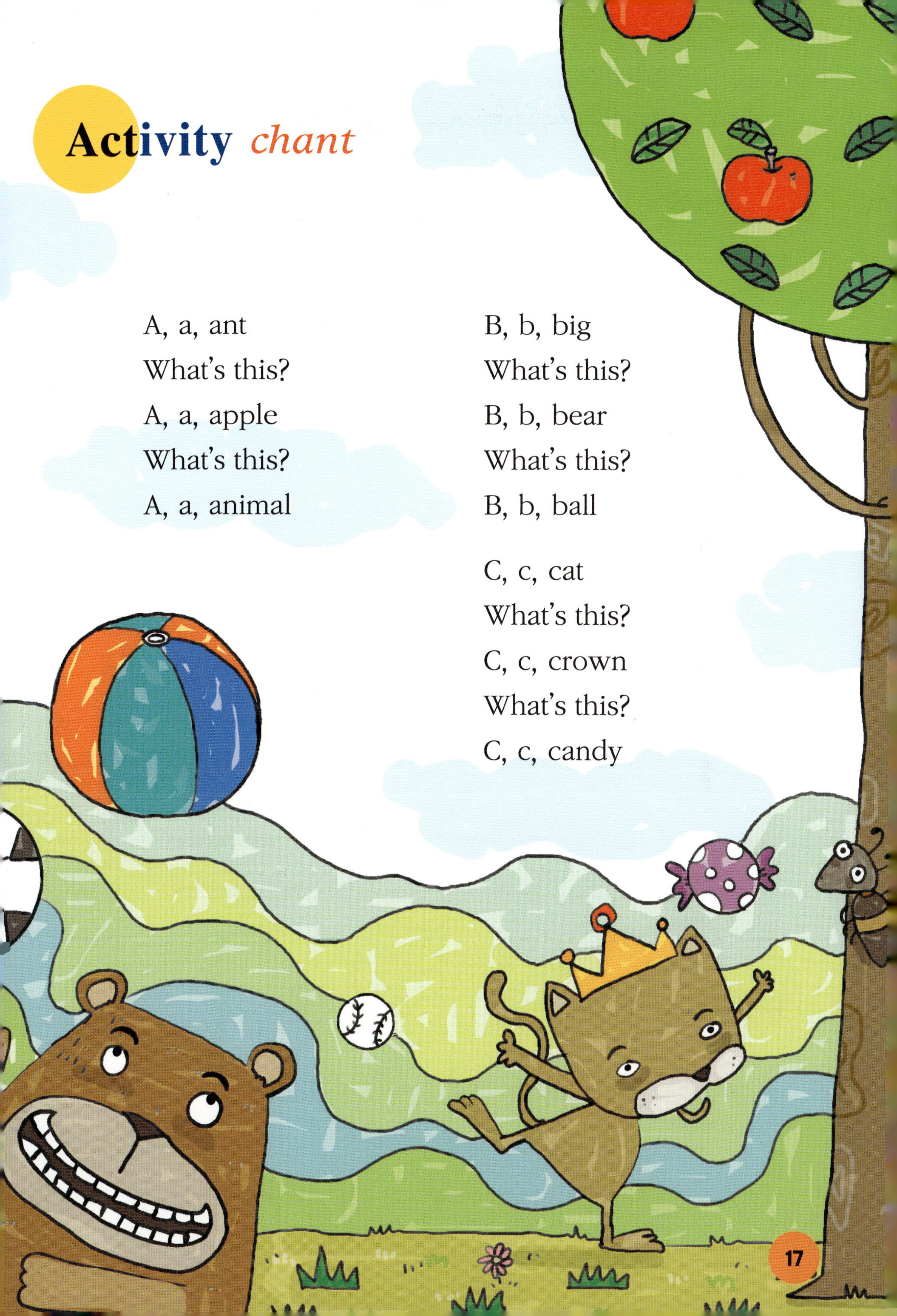

Activity chant

A, a, ant
What's this?
A, a, apple
What's this?
A, a, animal

B, b, big
What's this?
B, b, bear
What's this?
B, b, ball

C, c, cat
What's this?
C, c, crown
What's this?
C, c, candy

A dirty dog and a duck take the elevator.

An Eskimo and an elephant take the elevator.

A fork and a frog take the elevator.
Oh, the elevator is full.

Listen and repeat.

D d

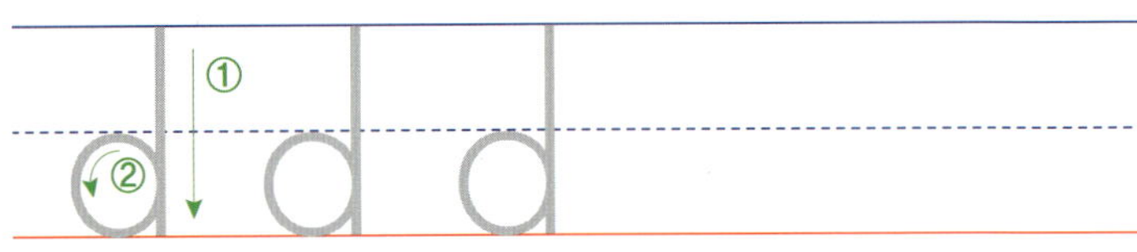

E e

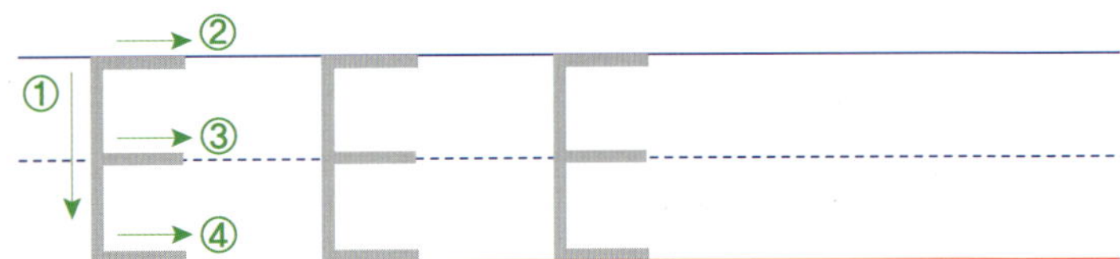

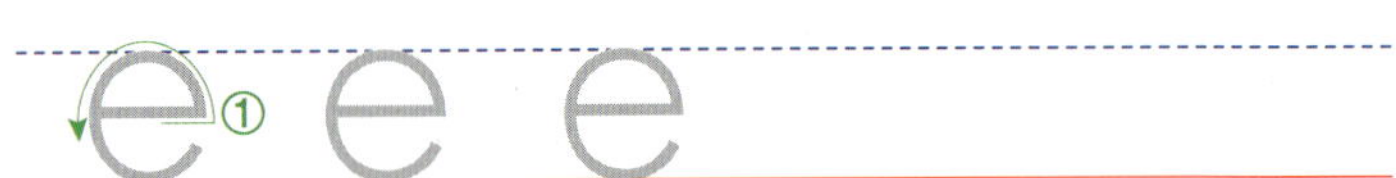

F f

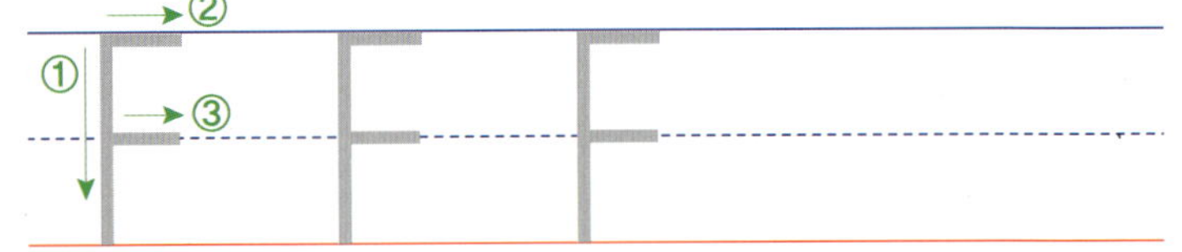

Listen, point and repeat.

D d	E e	F f
dirty	**E**skimo	**f**ork
dog	**e**lephant	**f**rog
duck	**e**levator	**f**ull

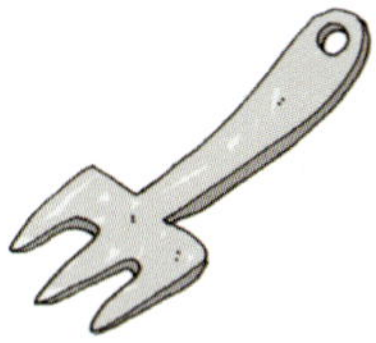

Listen to the beginning sound and circle
the correct picture.

1

2

3

4

Color the same sound with the same color.

Match the letter with the picture.

1. F f • • 

2. E e • • 

3. D d • • 

4. E e • • 

5. F f • • 

Find and complete the word.

1  [ ] u l l

2  [ ] u c k

3  [ ] s k i m o

4  [ ] o g

5 [ ] r o g

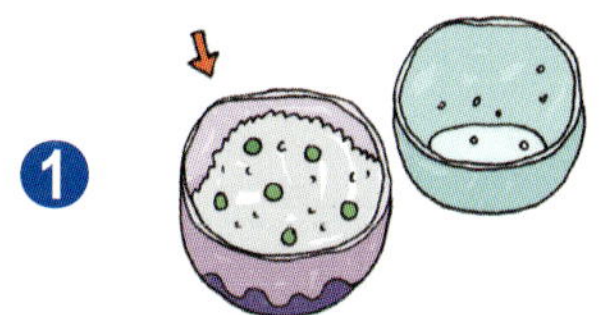

E b f d a c

Complete the crossword puzzle.

				1.						2.
				u						i
				l						r
			4.6.	l	e	p	h	a	n	t
			s							y
3.		o	r	k						
			i							
			m							
		5.	o	g						

Activity *chant*

It's dirty.
D, d, duck
D, d, dog.
It's a duck and a dog.

It's an Eskimo.
E, e, elephant.
E, e, elevator.
It's an elephant and an elevator.

It's full.
F, f, fotk
F, f, frog.
It's a fork and a frog.

A **g**orilla plays the **g**uitar
in the **g**arden.
A **h**en and a **h**orse
play on the **h**ill.
An **I**ndian and
an **i**guana play with
the **i**nsect.

Listen and repeat.

G g

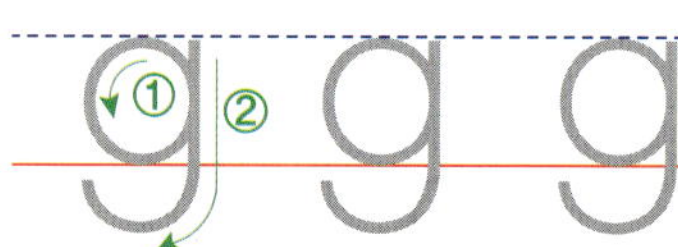

H h

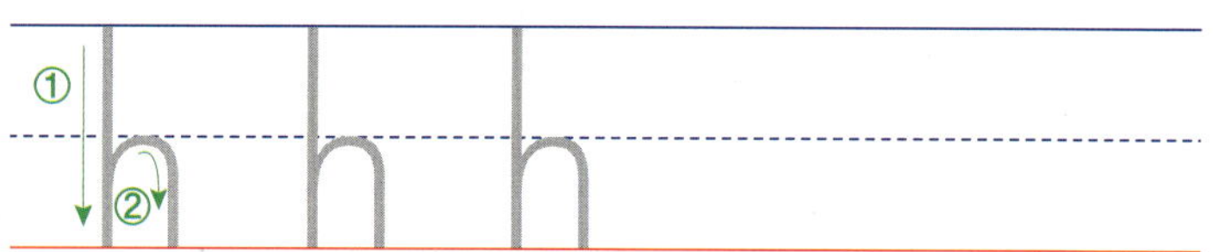

I i

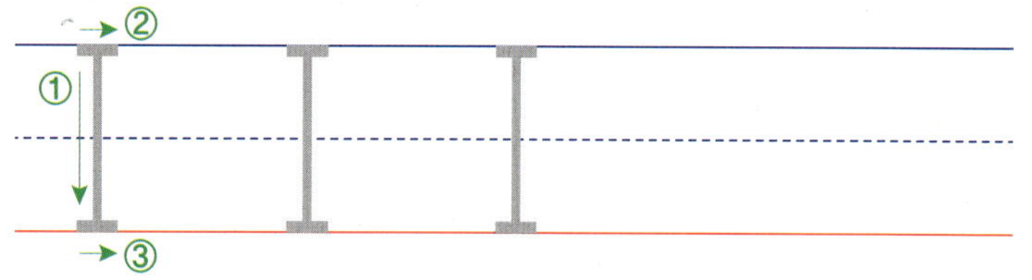

Listen, point and repeat.

G
g

gorilla

guitar

garden

H
h

hen

horse

hill

I
i

Indian

iguana

insect

Listen to the word and write the beginning letter.

1 

2 

3 

4 

5 

6 

7 

8 

9 

Color the same sound with the same color.

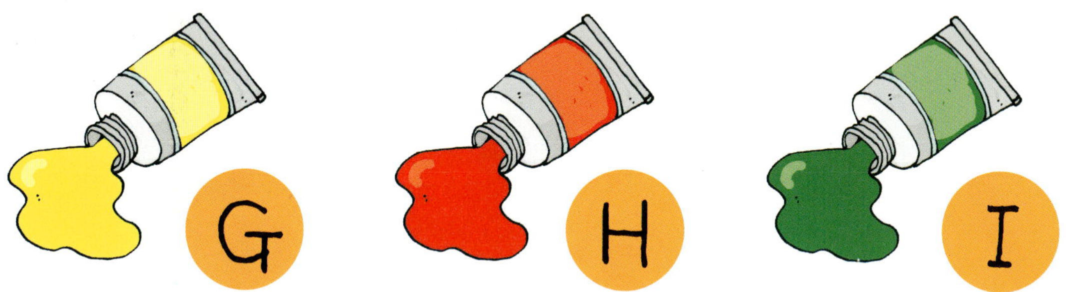

G H I

Practice – Read

Look at the picture and circle the correct letter.

1

Gg | Hh

2

Ii | Gg

3

Ii | Hh

4

Gg | Ii

5

Hh | Gg

6

Hh | Ii

Circle and write the beginning letter for the picture.

1 
G
H
I

2
G
H
I

3 
g
h
i

4
g
h
i

5 
G
H
I

6 
G
H
I

7 
g
h
i

8 
g
h
i

Complete the crossword puzzle.

G, g, G, g, guitar.
Where is the gorilla?
The gorilla is in the garden.

H, h, H, h, horse.
Where is the hen?
The hen is on the hill.

I, i, I, i, insect.
Where is the Indian?
The Indian is by the iguana.

Listen to the word and circle the correct picture.

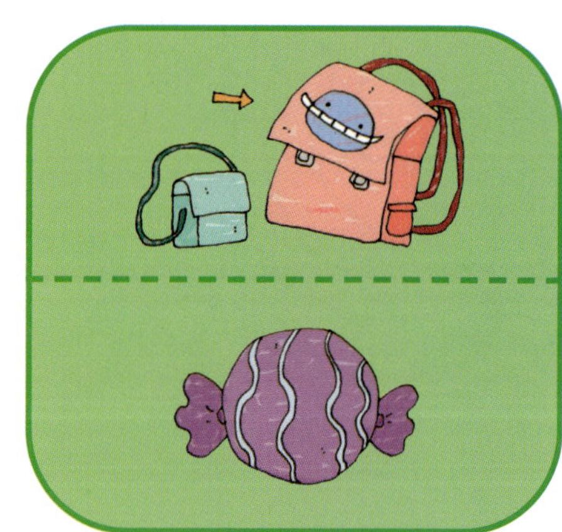

Circle the beginning letters.

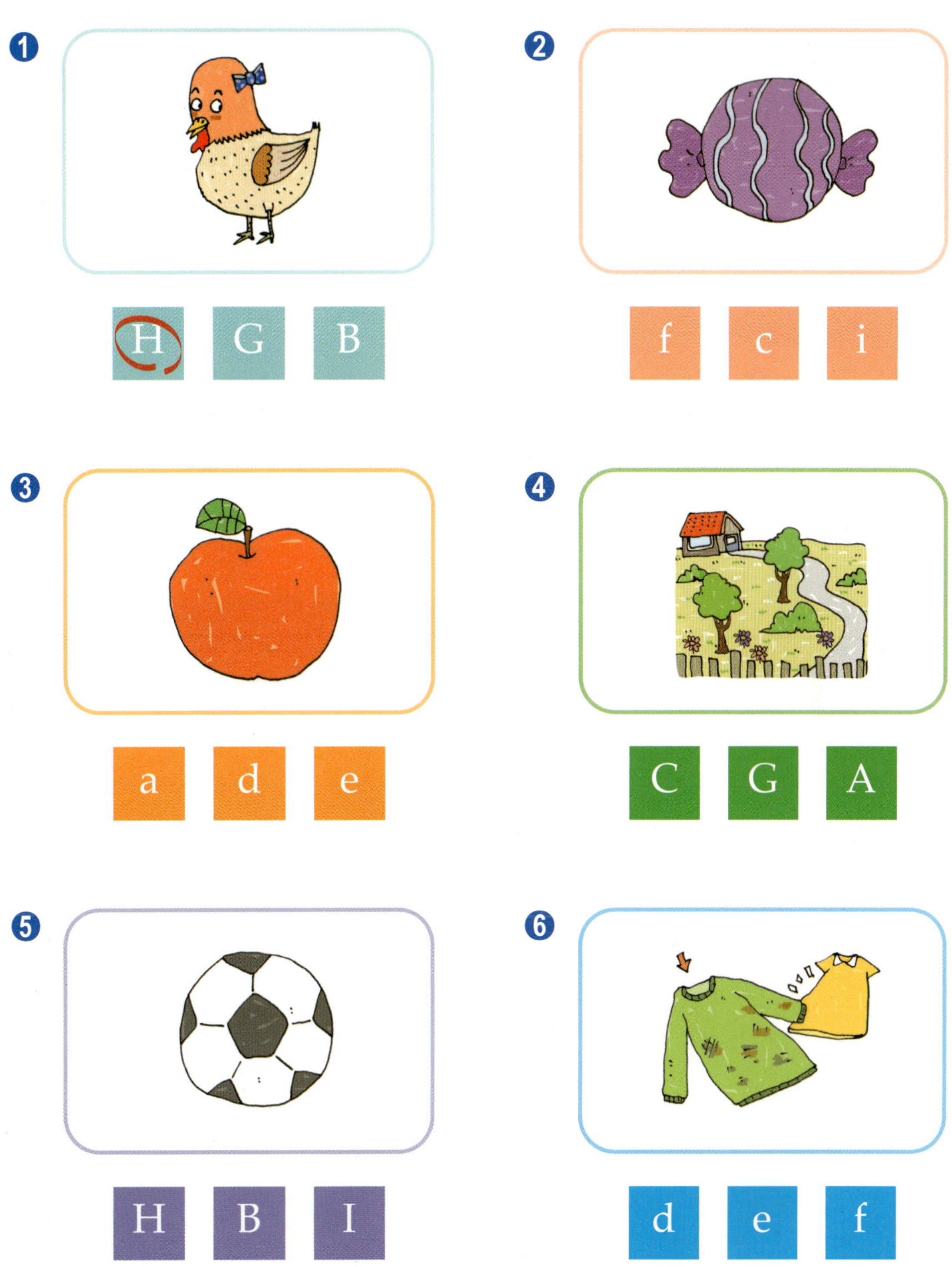

1. H G B

2. f c i

3. a d e

4. C G A

5. H B I

6. d e f

Find and circle the correct letters.

①  B I C F d h e i

②  A E D G c i f b

③  I F H C b a d e

④  C G A F d b e h

⑤  I H G E b c f a

Find and write the letter.

1 C at   **2** ☐ irty

3 ☐ uitar   **4** ☐ ill

5 ☐ levator   **6** ☐ nt

Unit 4 Alphabet Jj Kk Ll

A **j**eep is in the **j**ungle.
There is **j**am in the **j**eep.
A **k**angaroo **k**icks the **k**ettle
in the **j**ungle.
A **l**ion has a **l**amp and a **l**og
in the **j**ungle.

Listen and repeat.

J j

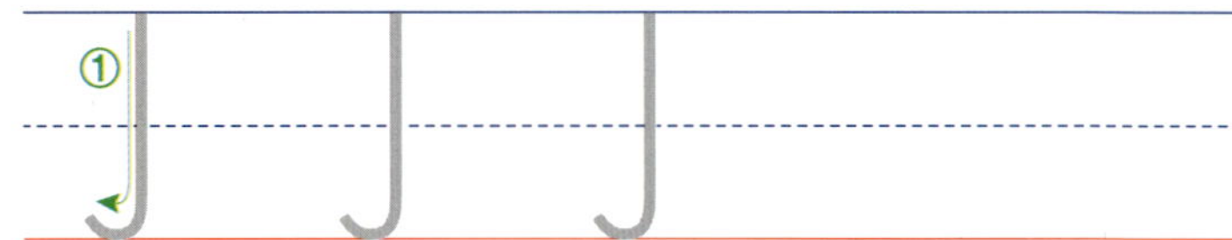

K k

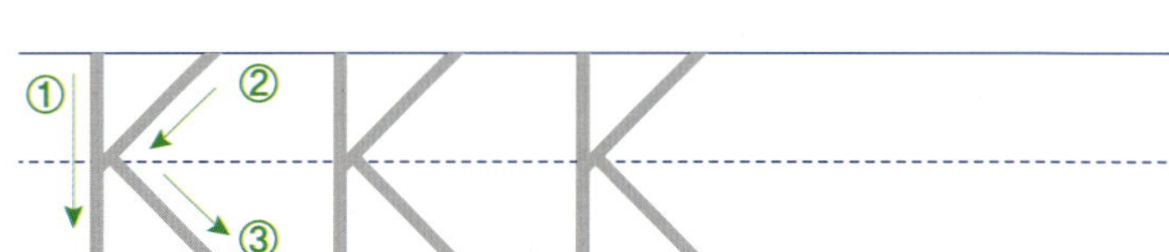

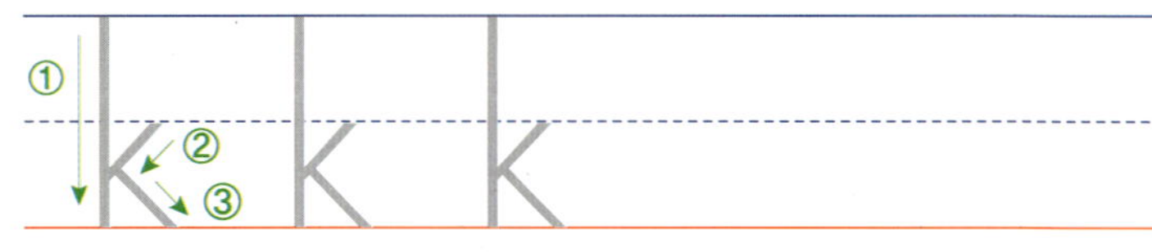

L l

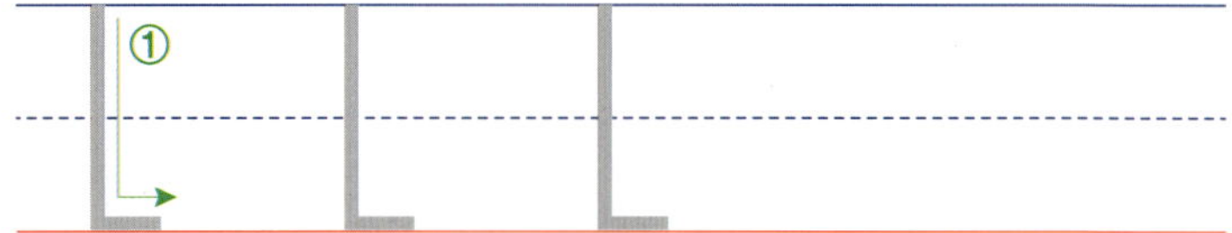

Listen, point and repeat.

| J | K | L |
| j | k | l |

jeep

jungle

jam

kangaroo

kick

kettle

lion

lamp

log

Practice – Listen

Listen and check the beginning sound letter.

1 j k l

2 j k l

3 j k l

4 j k l

5 j k l

6 j k l

Color the same sound with the same color.

Read and circle the correct picture.

 ①

L l

② **J j**

③ **K k**

④ **J j**

⑤ **L l**

Circle and write the missing letter.

1

__ a m

2

__ e t t l e

3

__ o g

4

__ i c k

5

__ e e p

6

__ i o n

Letter Search

Complete the crossword puzzle.

J, j, J, j, jungle
I have jam
J, j, J, j, jam
I have a jeep.
J, j, J, j, jeep.
…

K, k, K, k, kick
I have a kangaroo.
K, k, K, k, kangaroo
I have a kettle.
K, k, K, k, kettle
L, l, L, l, lion
I have a lamp.
L, l, L, l, lamp
I have a log.
L, l, L, l, log

A monkey makes a mask.
Nine nuts make a net.
An octopus makes an omelet
with an ostrich.

Listen and repeat.

M m

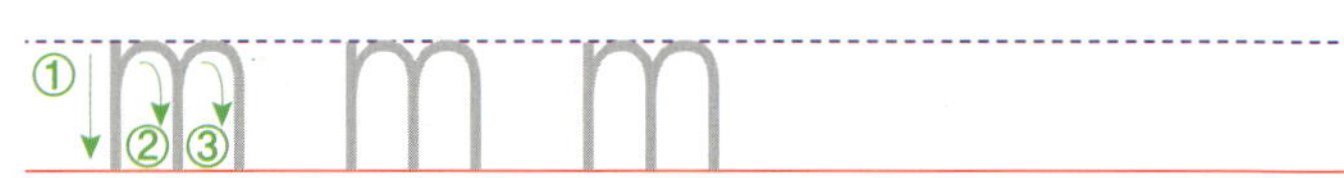

N n

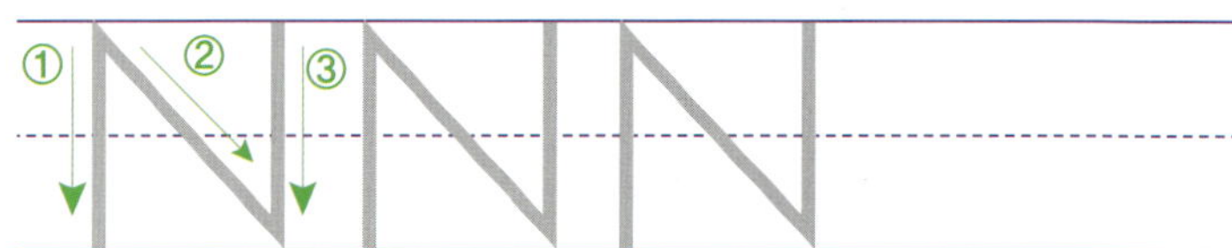

O o

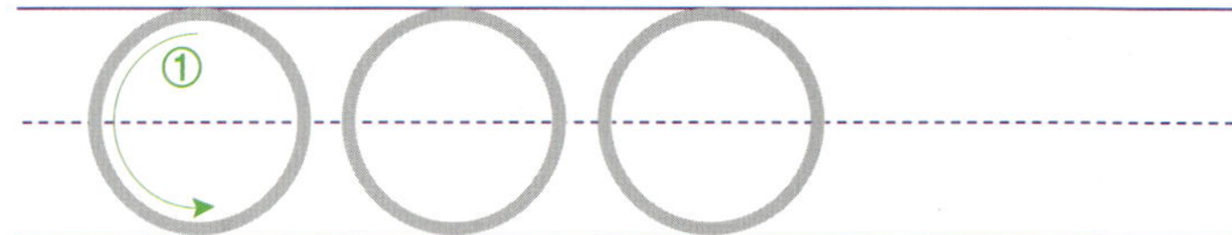

Listen, point and repeat.

M
m

monkey

make

mask

N
n

nine

nut

net

O
o

octopus

omelet

ostrich

Listen to the beginning sound and circle
the correct picture.

1  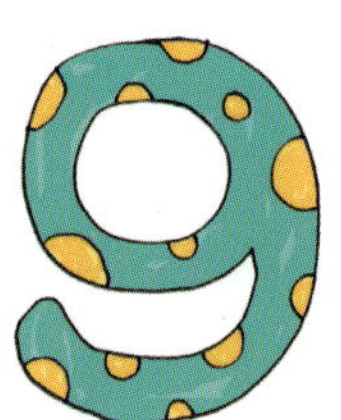 

2   

3 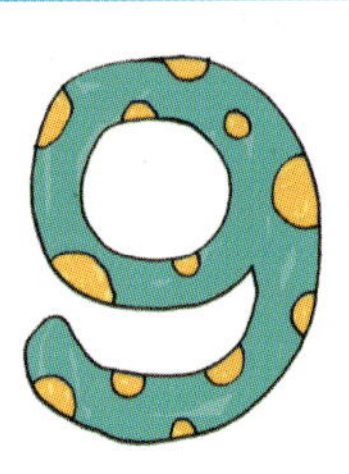  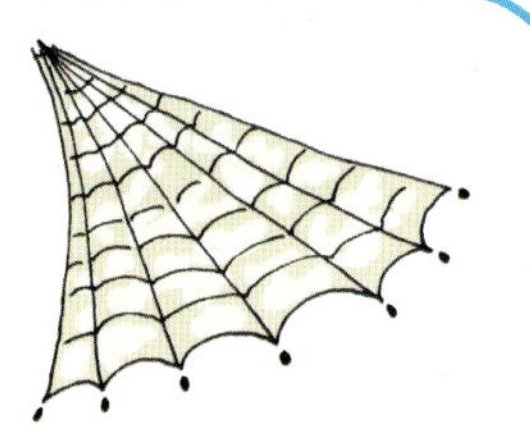

4   

Color the same sound with the same color.

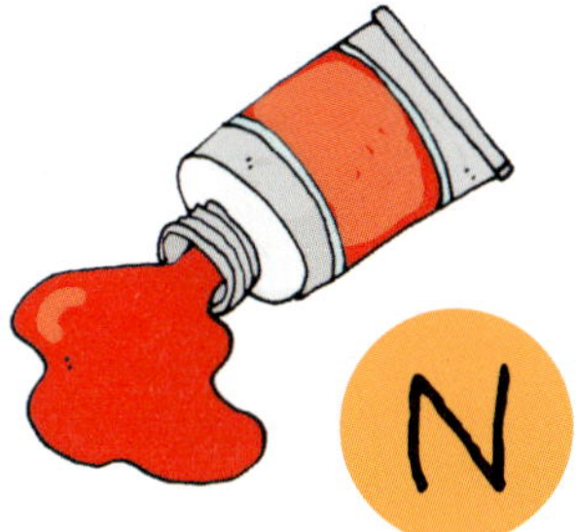

Match the letter with the picture.

① N n

② O o

③ M m

④ N n

⑤ O o

Find and complete the word.

1.  ☐ m e l e t

2.  ☐ a s k

3.  ☐ e t

4.  ☐ i n e

5. ☐ a k e

l n i o k m h

Complete the crossword puzzle.

		1.			2.4.		
						a	k	e
		u			a		
5.		c	t	3.	p	u	s	
			m			k		
			e					
			l					
			e					
	6.		e	t				

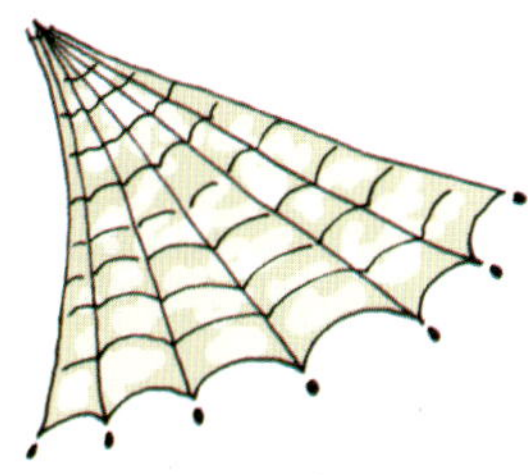

M, m, M, m make!
Who am I?
I have a mask.
Monkey, monkey, monkey.

N, n, N, n nine!
Who am I?
I have a net.
Nut, nut, nut.

O, o, O, o ostrich!
Who am I?
I have an omelet.
Octopus, octopus, octopus.

Unit 6 Alphabet Pp Qq Rr

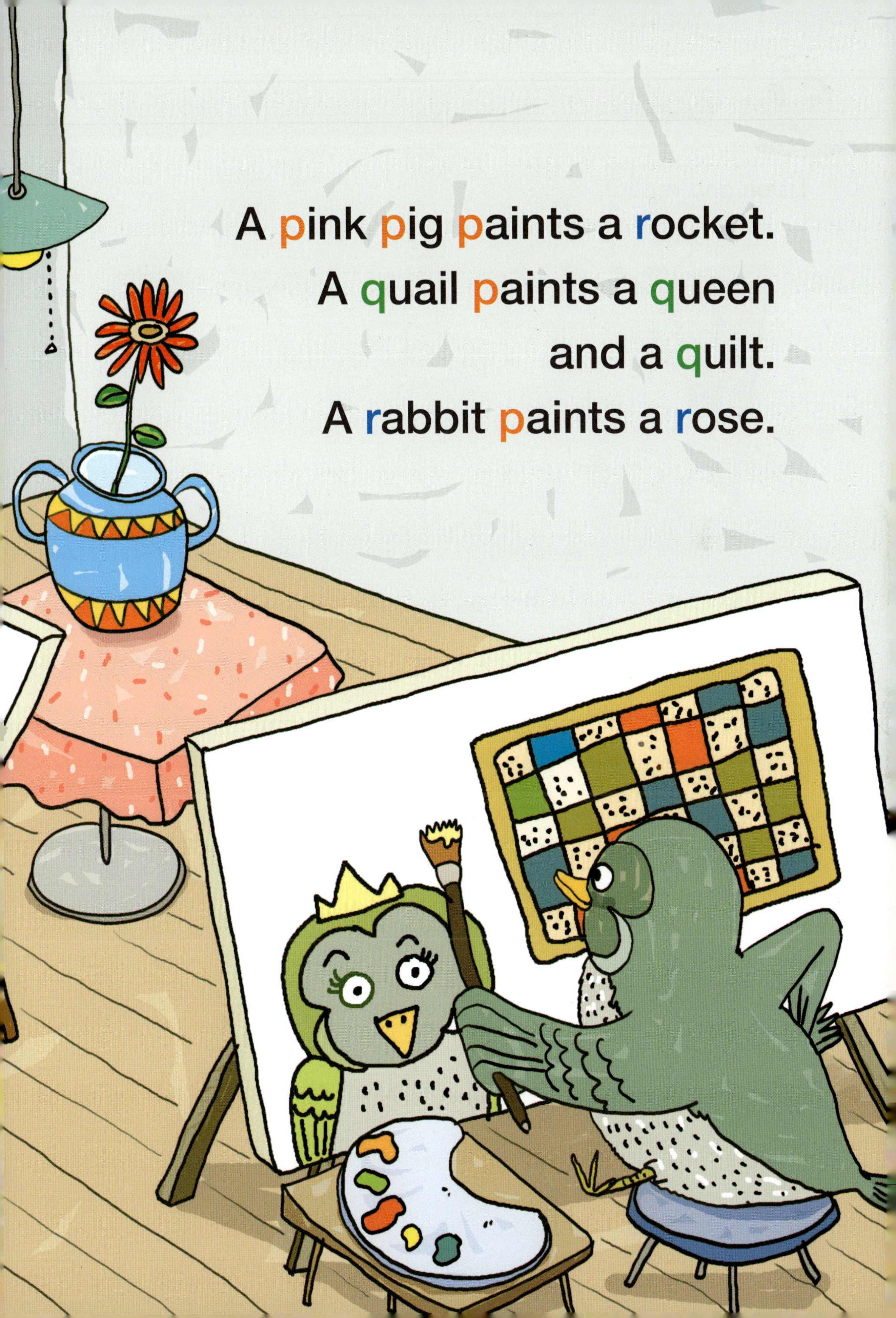

A pink pig paints a rocket.
A quail paints a queen
and a quilt.
A rabbit paints a rose.

Listen and repeat.

P p

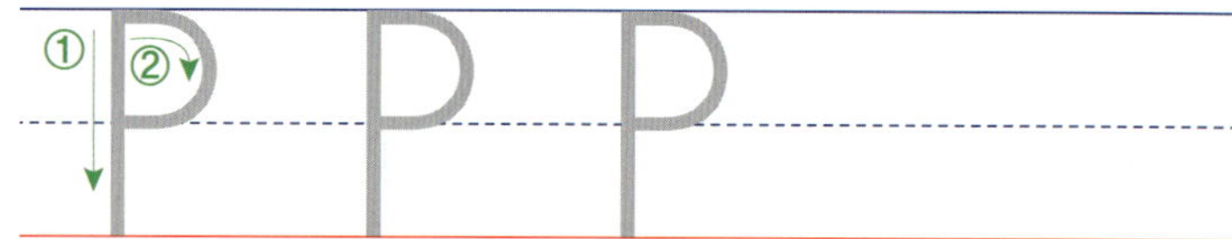

Q q

R r

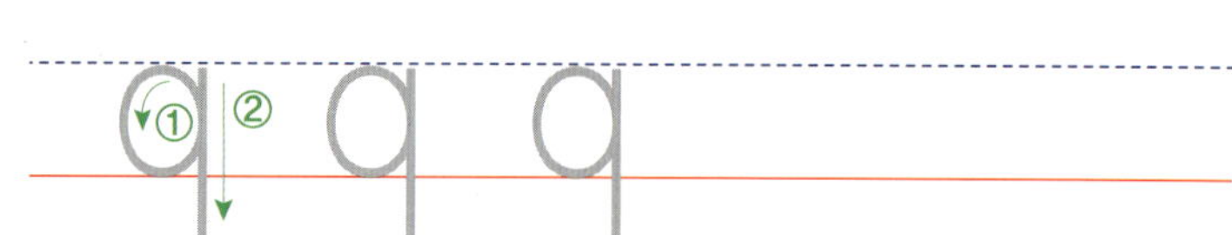

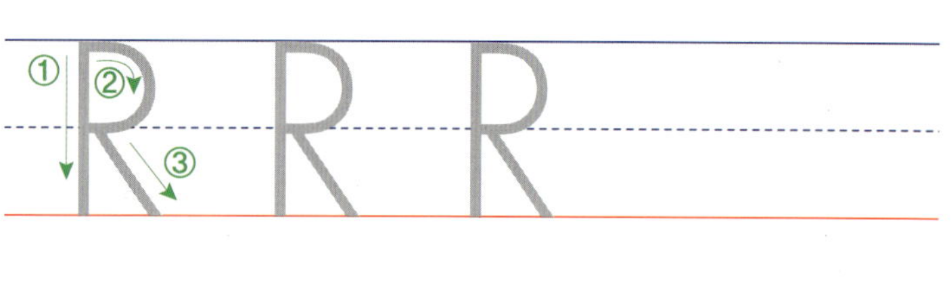

Listen, point and repeat.

P
p

paint

pig

pink

Q
q

quail

queen

quilt

R
r

rocket

rabbit

rose

Listen to the word and write the beginning letter.

1 

2 

3 

4 

5 

6 

7 

8 

9 

Color the same sound with the same color.

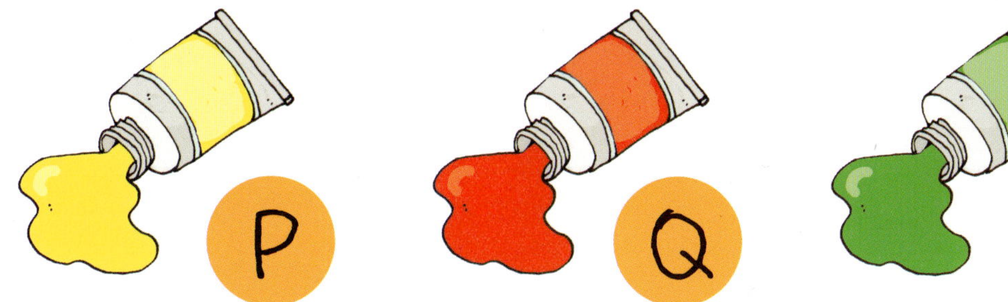

Practice – Read

Look at the picture and circle the correct letter.

1 Qq | Rr

2 Rr | Pp

3 Pp | Qq

4 Rr | Qq

5 Rr | Pp

6 Qq | Pp

Circle and write the beginning letter for the picture.

1. P Q R

2. P Q R

3. p q r

4. p q r

5. P Q R

6. P Q R

7. p q r

8. p q r

Letter Search

Complete the crossword puzzle.

1 
2 
3 

4 
5 
6 

 Activity *chant*

P, p, P, p, pink.
P, p, P, p, pig.
Look! A pink pig!
Not paint!
Q, q, Q, q, quail.
Q, q, Q, q, quilt.
Look! A quail on the quilt!
Not on the queen!

R, r, R, r, rabbit.
R, r, R, r, rocket.
Look! A rabbit in the rocket!
Not in the roses!

Review 2

Listen to the word and circle the correct picture.

① 

② 

③ 

④ 

⑤ 

⑥ 

Circle the beginning letters.

Match and write the small letter.

1. M

2. Q

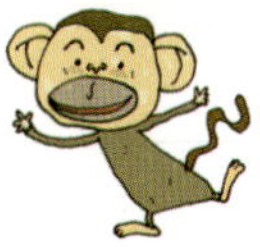

3. K

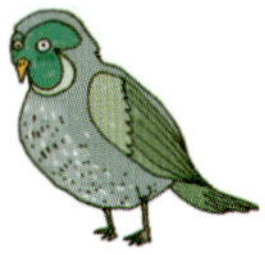

4. O

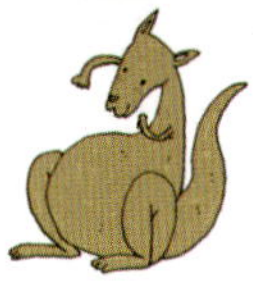

5. J

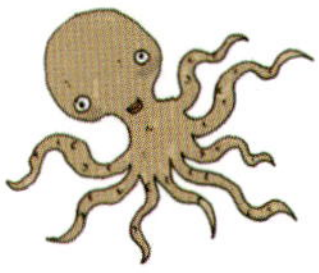

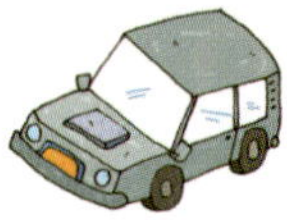

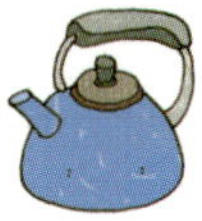

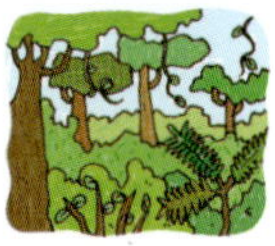

m

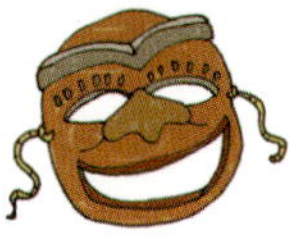

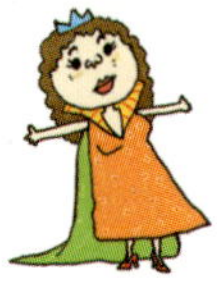

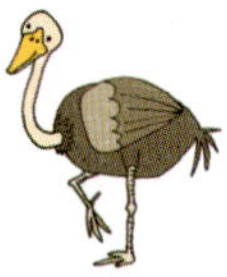

Find and write the beginning letter for the picture.

log   kettle   nine   omelet

queen   lion   rose   pink

Unit 7 Alphabet Ss Tt Uu

A seal sings in the sea.
Twin tigers sing between the trees.
An ugly uncle sings
with an umbrella.

Listen and repeat.

S s

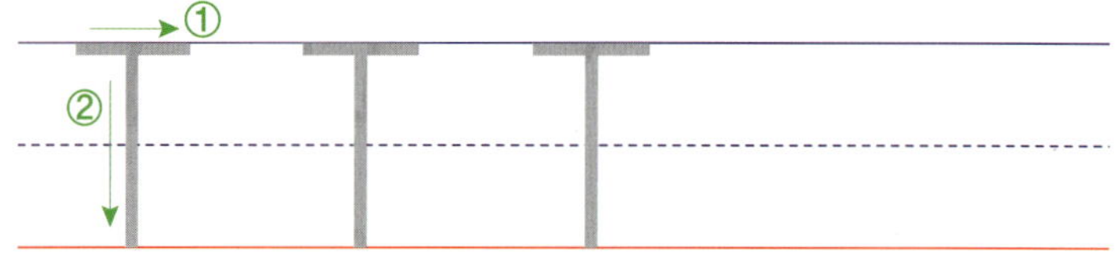

T t

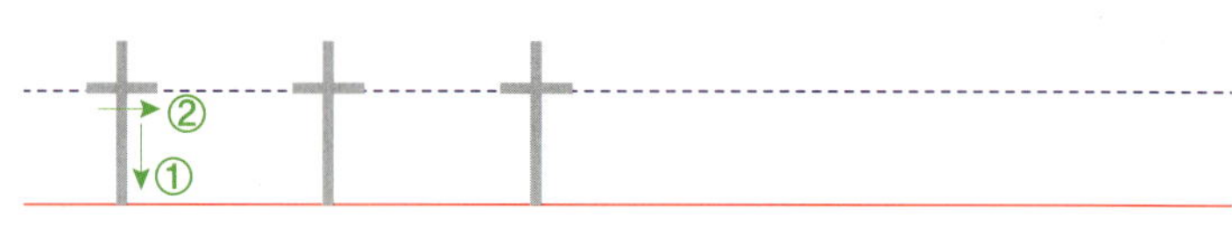

U u

Listen, point and repeat.

S s	T t	U u

seal

sing

sea

twins

tiger

tree

ugly

uncle

umbrella

Practice – Listen

Listen and check the beginning sound letter.

1

s t u

2

s t u

3

s t u

4

s t u

5

s t u

6

s t u

Color the same sound with the same color.

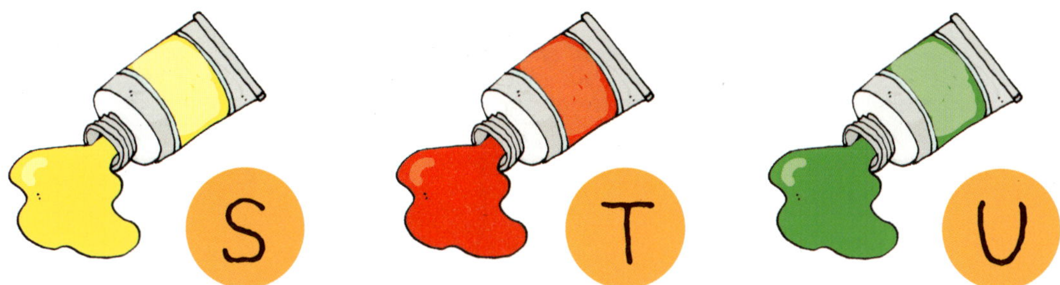

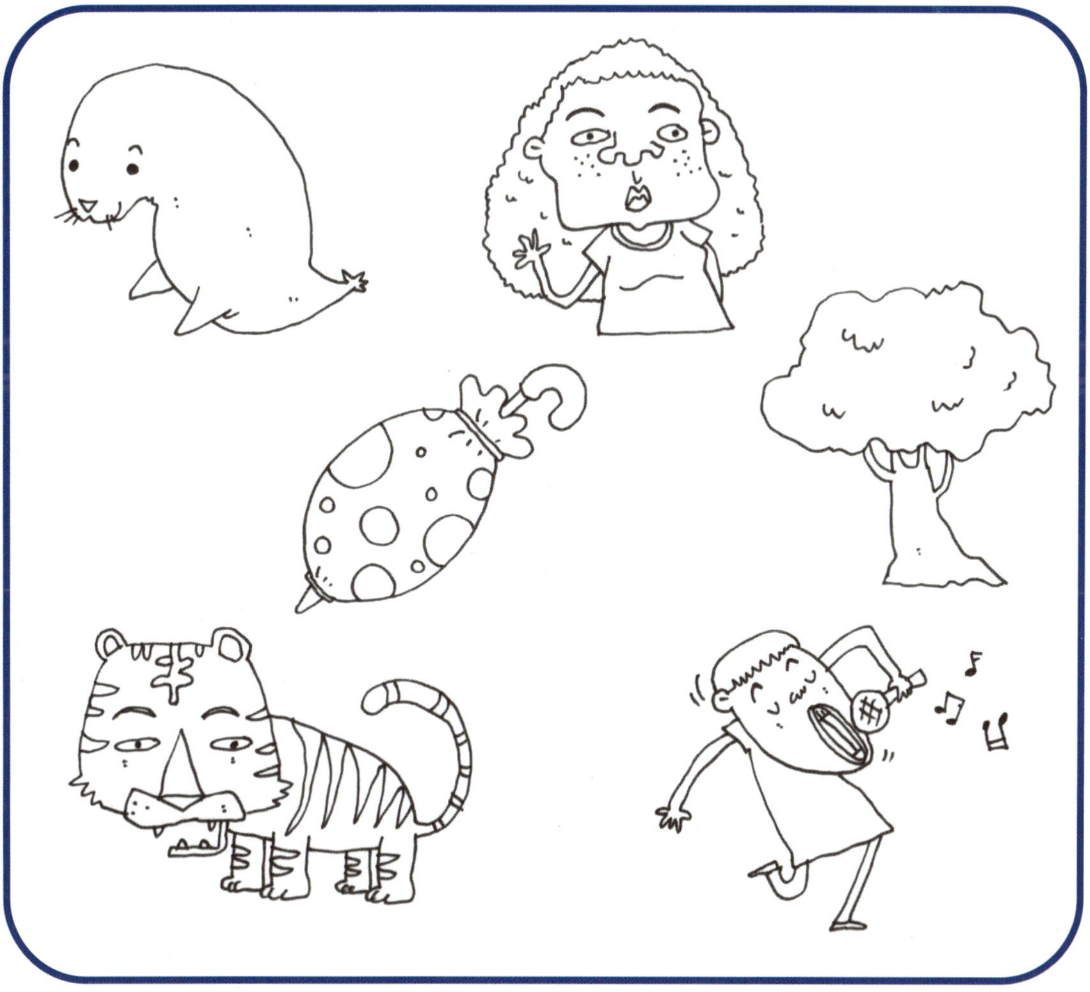

Read and circle the correct picture.

1 S s     

2 T t     

3 T t     

4 U u     

5 S s     

Circle and write the missing letter.

1

s
t
u

__ i g e r

2

s
t
u

__ m b r e l l a

3

s
t
u

__ e a

4

s
t
u

__ i n g

5

s
t
u

__ g l y

6

s
t
u

__ r e e

Complete the crossword puzzle.

❶ 

❷ 

❸ 

					1.				5.
		3.	w	i	n				
				g					e
4.6.		m	b	r	e	l	l	a	
n				r				l	
c									
l									
2. e	a								

❹ 

❺ 

❻ 

S, s, Sing.
What's your name?
I'm a S, s, seal.
What's your name?
I'm a S, s, sea.

T, t, twin.
What's your name?
I'm a T, t, tiger.
What's your name?
I'm a T, t, tree.

U, u, ugly.
What's your name?
I'm an U, u, uncle.
What's your name?
I'm an U, u, umbrella.

A **v**ulture has a **v**ane.
A **w**olf has a **w**et **w**ig
and a **v**est.
Si**x** fo**x**es have the bo**x**.

Listen and repeat.

V v

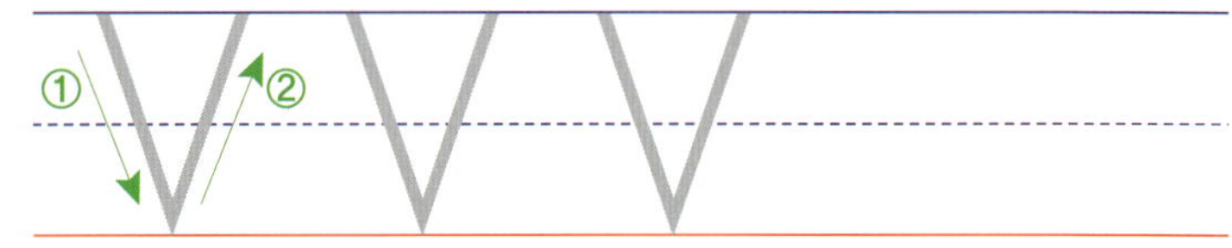

W w

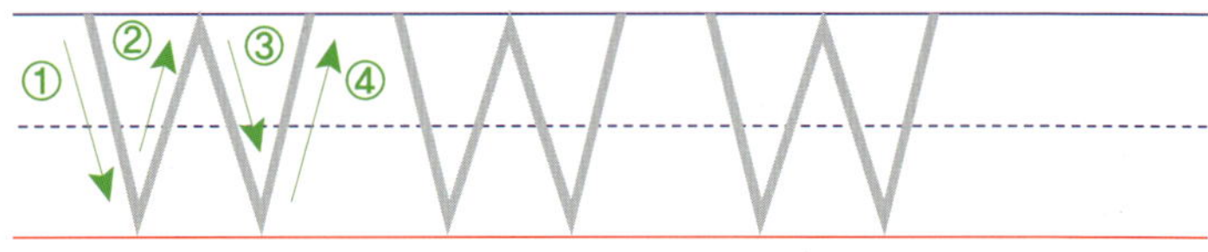

X x

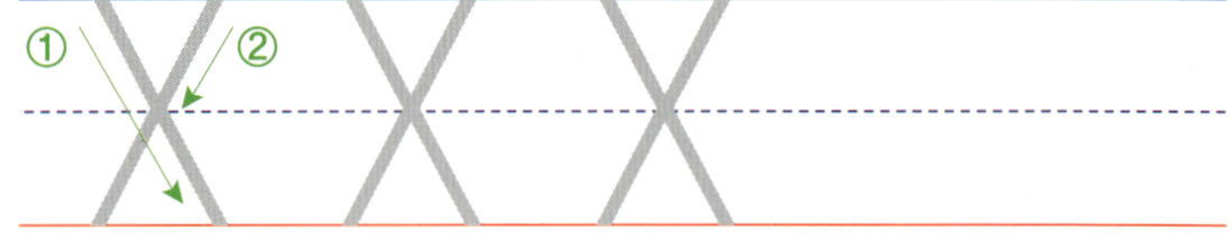

Listen, point and repeat.

V v	W w	X x
vulture	wolf	six
vane	wet	fox
vest	wig	box

Practice – Listen

Listen to the beginning(ending) sound and circle
the correct picture.

1 

2 

3 

4 

Color the same sound with the same color.

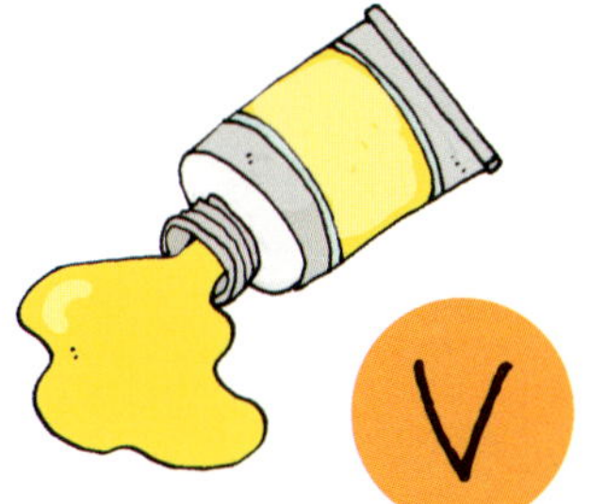

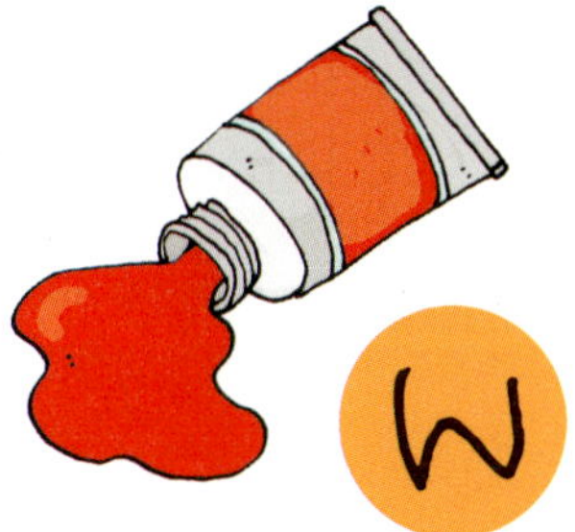

Match the letter with the picture.

① **X x** •   • 

② **V v** •   • 

③ **W w** •   • 

④ **X x** •   • 

⑤ **V v** •   • 

Find and complete the word.

1.  | | e | s | t |

2.  | | o | l | f |

3.  | | e | t |

4.  | f | o | |

5.  | | a | n | e |

| s | x | t | v | u | w | r |

Complete the crossword puzzle.

1  **2**  **3** 

<table>
<tr><td></td><td></td><td></td><td></td><td></td><td>5.</td><td></td><td></td></tr>
<tr><td>1.</td><td>u</td><td>l</td><td>t</td><td>u</td><td>r</td><td>e</td><td></td></tr>
<tr><td></td><td></td><td></td><td></td><td></td><td>2. s</td><td>i</td><td></td></tr>
<tr><td></td><td></td><td></td><td>3.4.</td><td></td><td>e</td><td>t</td><td></td></tr>
<tr><td></td><td></td><td></td><td>o</td><td></td><td></td><td></td><td></td></tr>
<tr><td></td><td></td><td></td><td>l</td><td></td><td></td><td></td><td></td></tr>
<tr><td></td><td></td><td></td><td>6. f</td><td>o</td><td></td><td></td><td></td></tr>
</table>

4  **5**  **6** 

Activity *chant*

ZOO

A yak yells in the zoo.
A zero and a zebra yawn
in the zoo.

Listen and repeat.

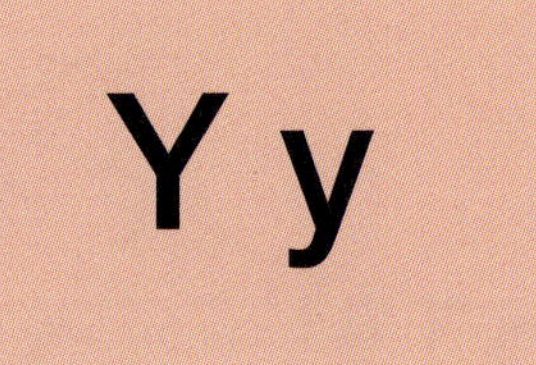

Y y

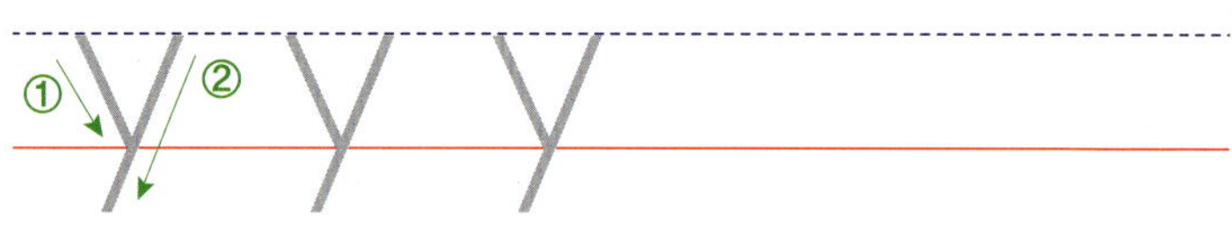

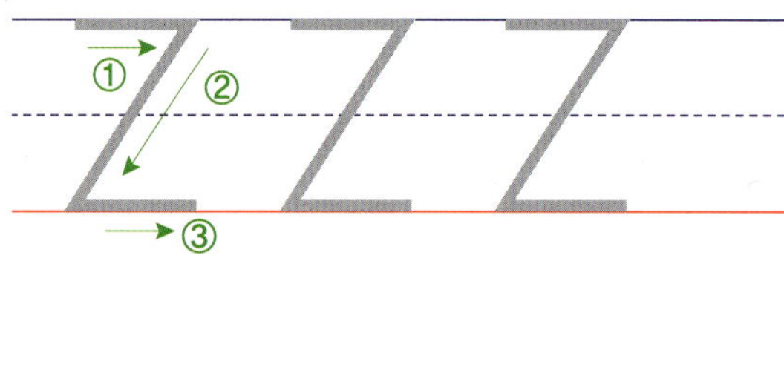

Z z

Listen, point and repeat.

Y
y

yak

yell

yawn

Z
z

zoo

zero

zebra

Practice – Listen

Listen to the word and write the beginning letter.

1 

2 

3 

4 

5 

6 

Color the same sound with the same color.

Look at the picture and chcek the correct letter.

1

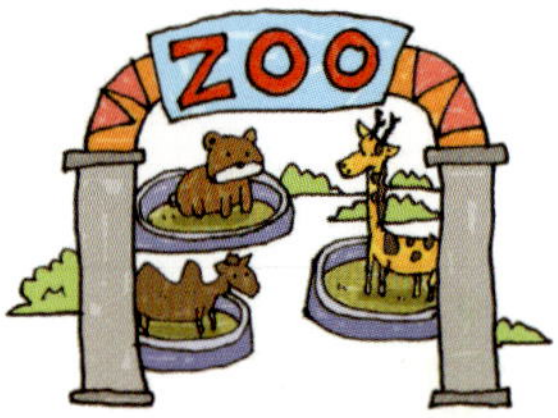

Yy | Zz

2

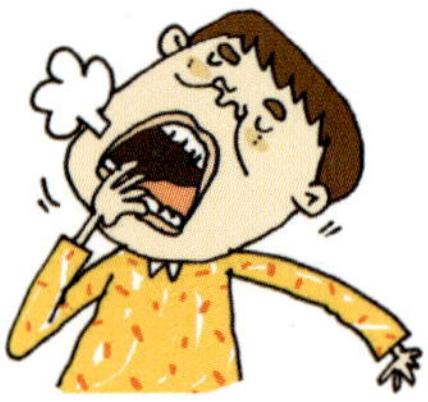

Yy | Zz

3

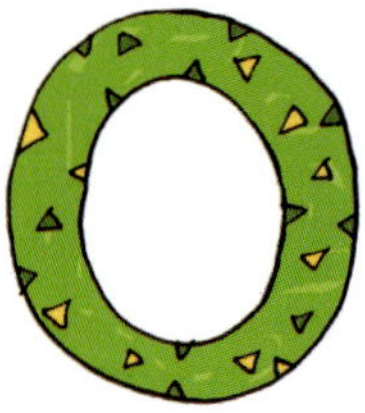

Yy | Zz

4

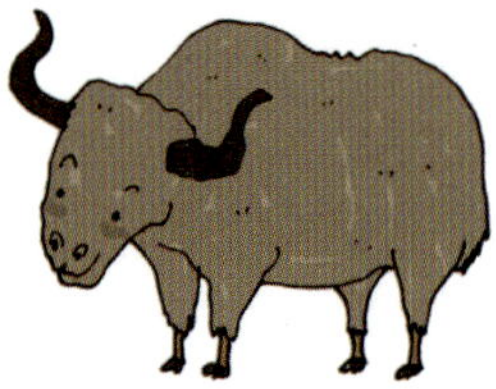

Yy | Zz

5

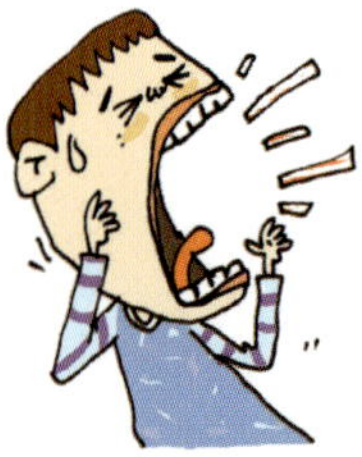

Yy | Zz

6

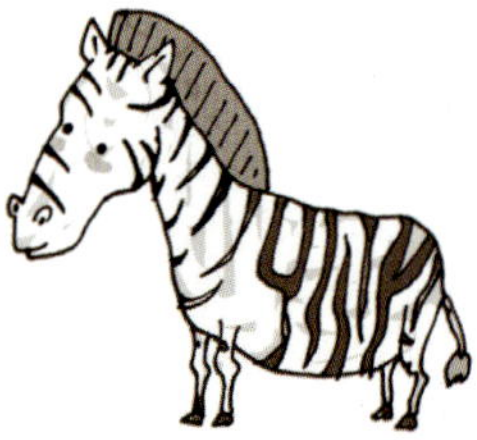

Yy | Zz

Circle and write the beginning letter for the picture.

1 
Y
Z

2 
Y
Z

3 
y
z

4 

y
z

5 
Y
Z

6 
y
z

Complete the crossword puzzle.

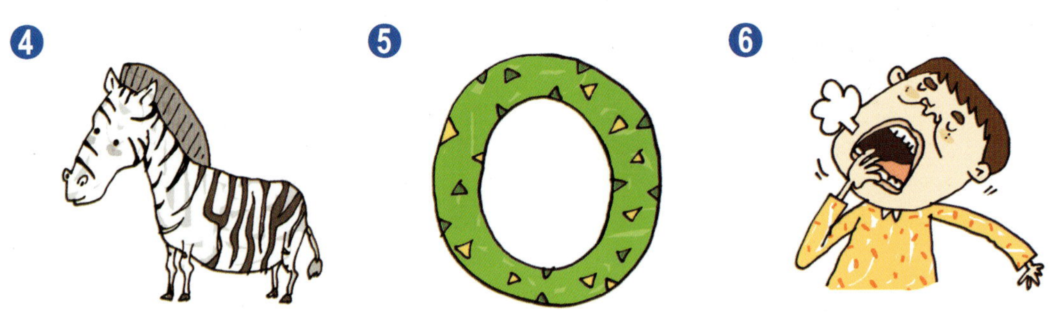

Y, y, yell.
Y, y, yawn.
What do you have?
I have a Y, y, yak.

Z, z, Zoo.
What do you have?
I have Z, z, Zero.
What do you have?
I have a Z, z, zebra.

Listen and circle the right picture.

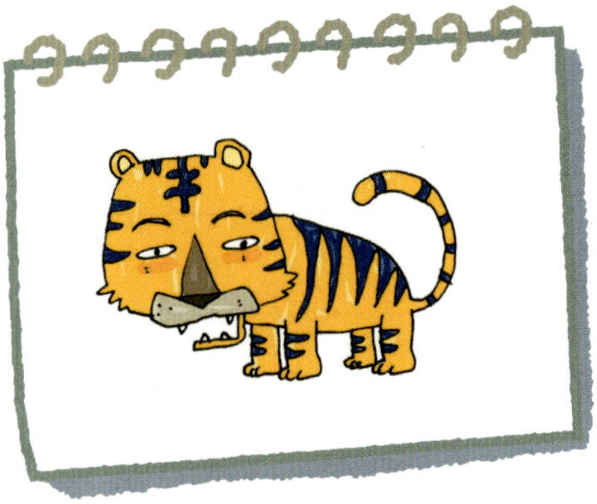

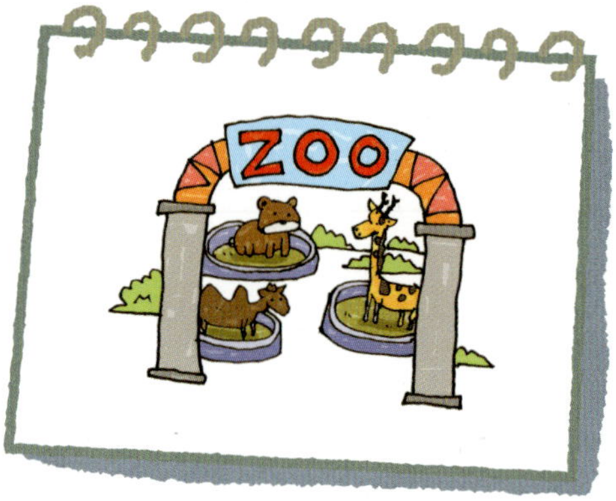

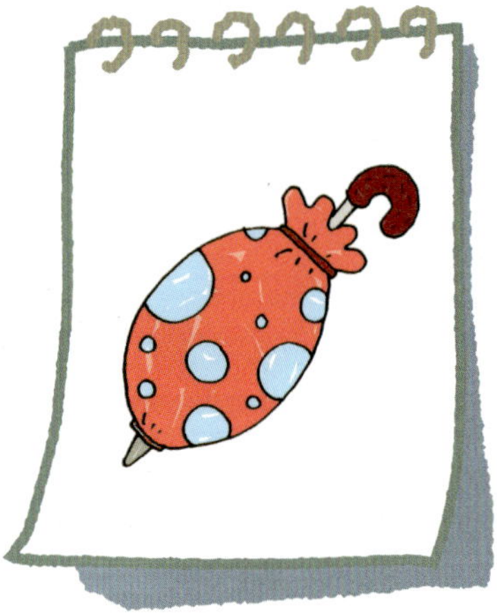

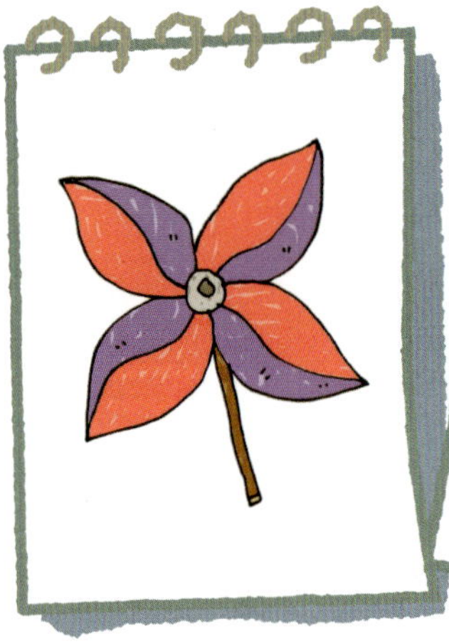

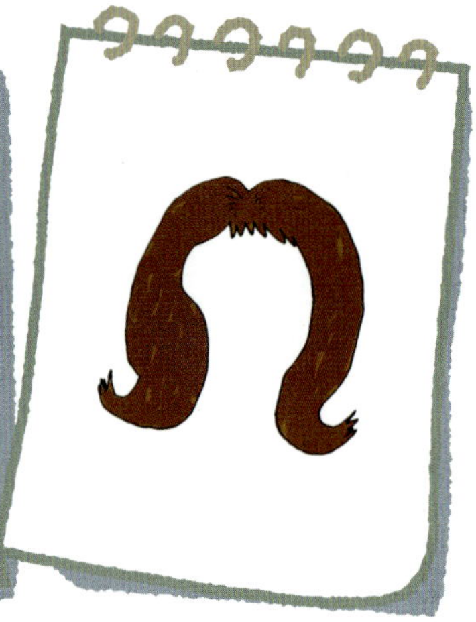

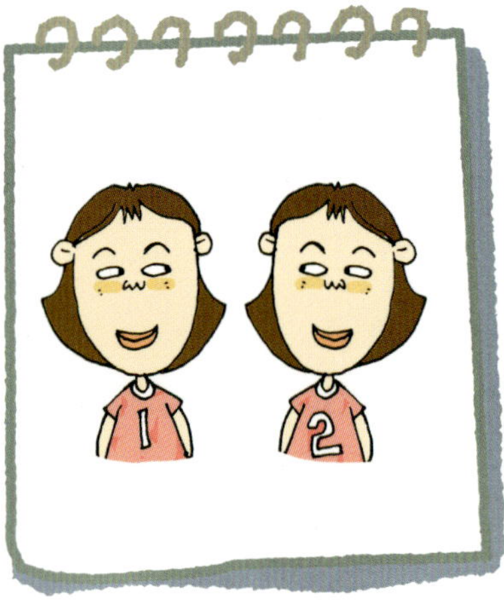

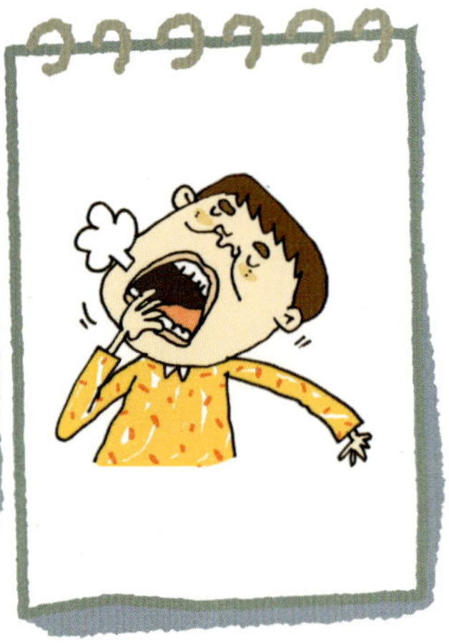

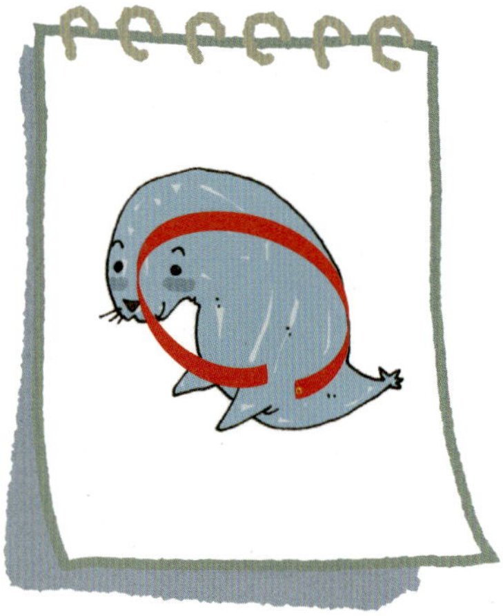

Circle the right match.

1
W
w

Z
z

S
s

2
V
v
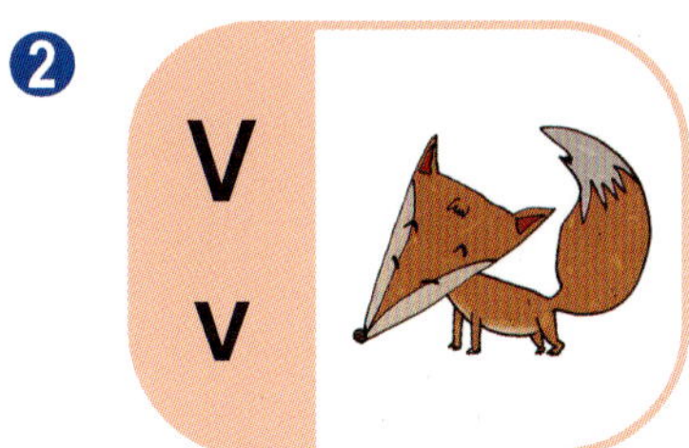
Y
y

T
t

3
X
x
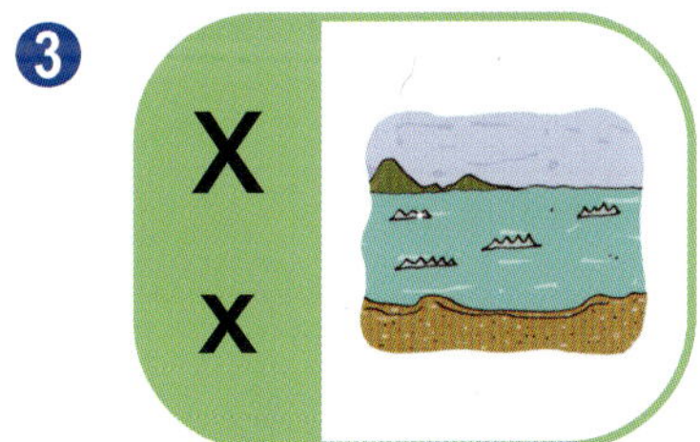
W
w

U
u

4
S
s

Y
y

Z
z

Circle and complete the words.

1

u
t

__U__ n c l e

2

v
w

__ i g

3

w
y

__ e l l

4

x
z

f o __

5

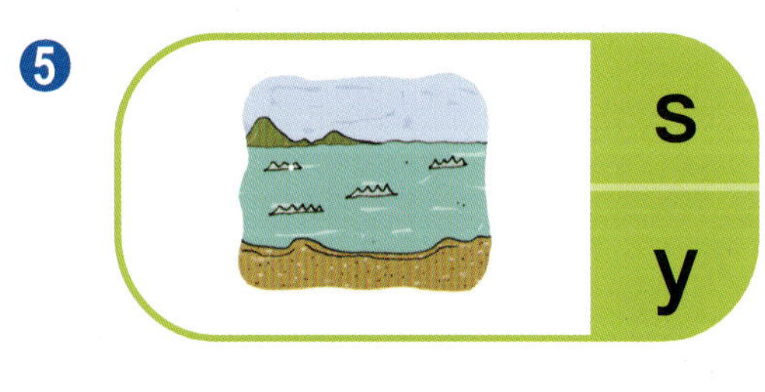

s
y

__ e a

6

v
u

__ e s t

7

t
x

__ i g e r

8

__ o o

Write the letter in the correct box.

Tt	Xx	Yy	Ww
Xx	Tt	Yy	Ww

1 si x

2 olf

3 bo

4 ree

5 ak

6 awn

7 ig

8 iger

Test

Listen and circle the beginning letters.

1 Rr　Bb　Kk　Xx

2 Qq　Mm　Ii　Ff

3 Zz　Jj　Uu　Aa

4 Hh　Pp　Dd　Nn

5 Oo　Ll　Ss　Ee

Listen and circle the T or F.

Test

Match the pictures with the same beginning sounds.

① 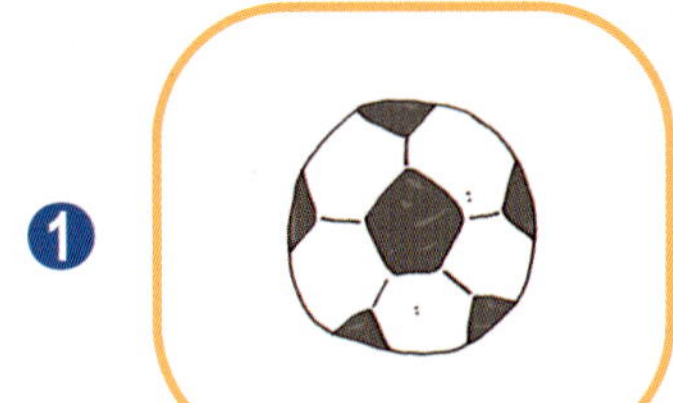 ──────────── 

②  

③ 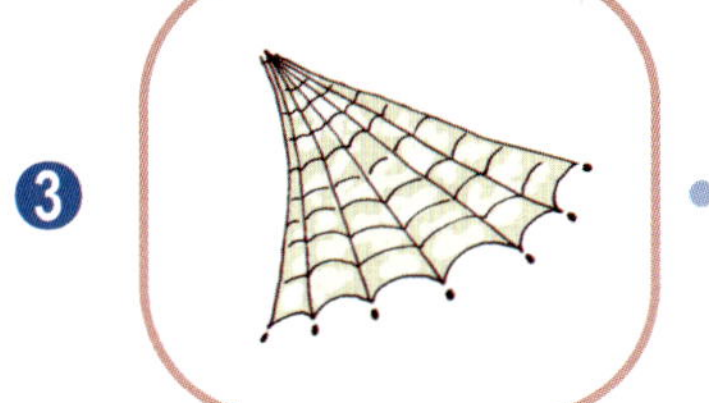 

④  

⑤  

Circle the picture with a different beginning sound.

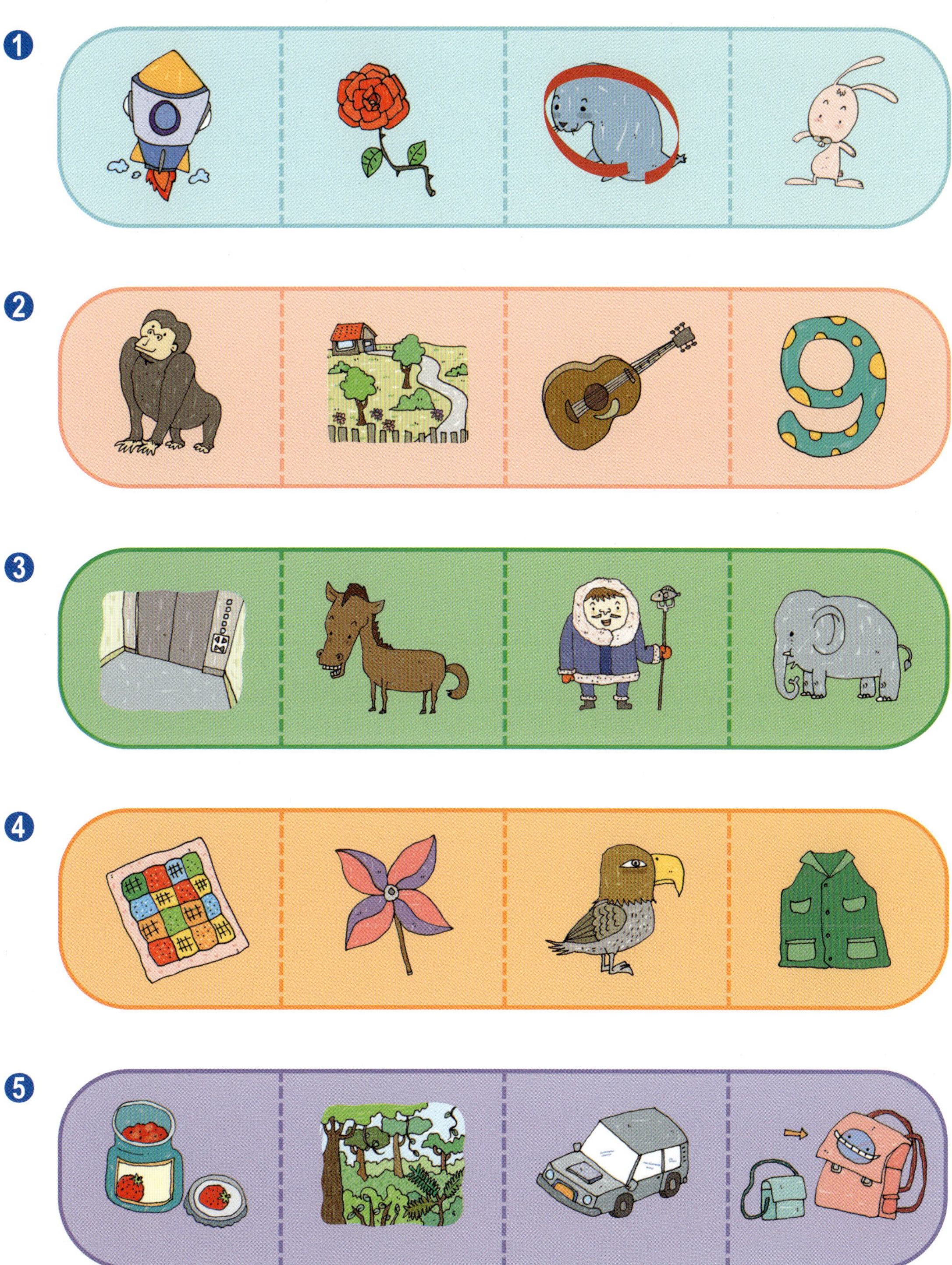

Test

Find the correct letter for the picture.

ⓐ Oo ✔   ⓑ Qq   ⓒ Aa

ⓐ Nn   ⓑ Kk   ⓒ Mm

ⓐ Ee   ⓑ Ii   ⓒ Uu

ⓐ Bb   ⓑ Gg   ⓒ Aa

ⓐ Dd   ⓑ Pp   ⓒ Ff

Look, circle and write the letters.

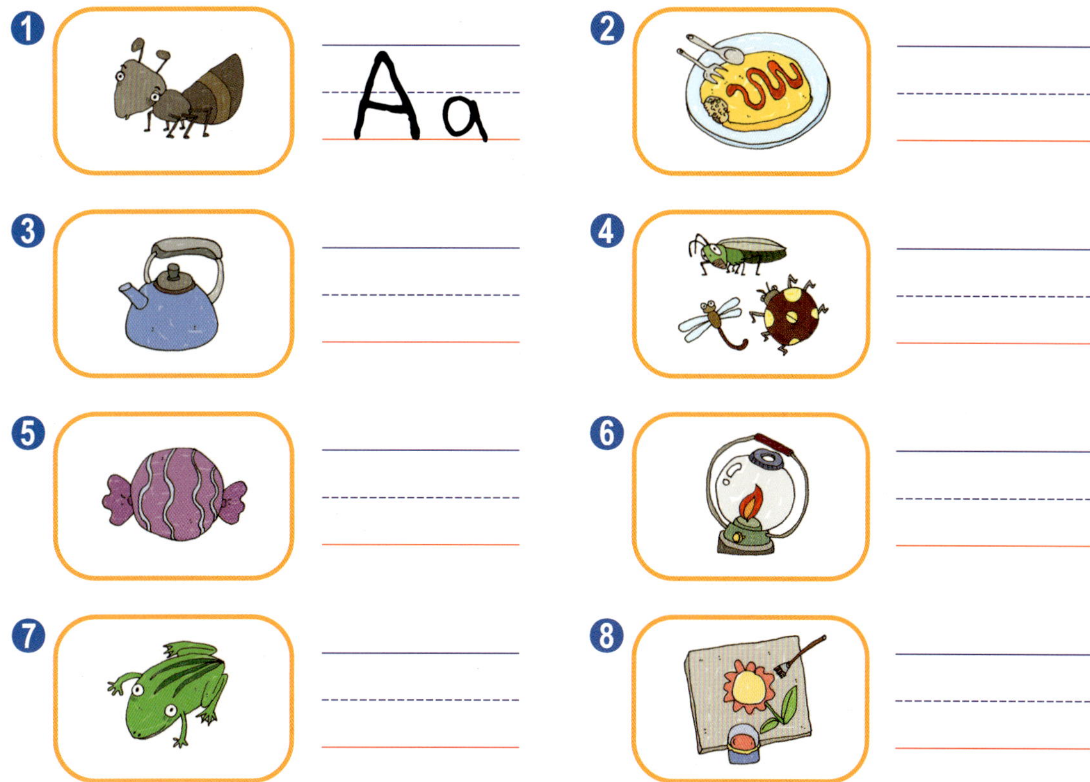

Answer Key

12p
❶ b
❷ c
❸ a
❹ c
❺ b
❻ a

13p

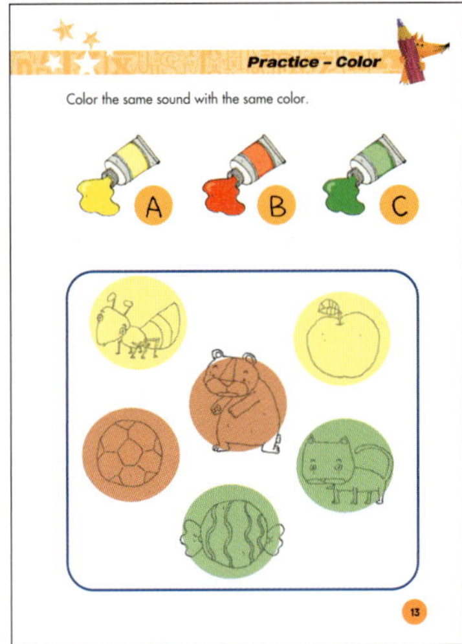

14p

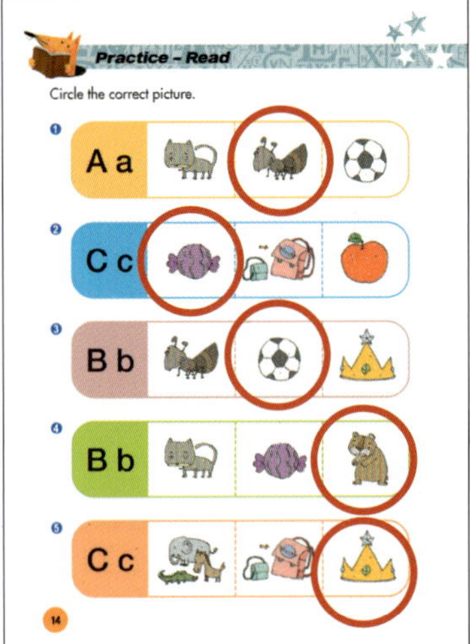

15p
❶ b
❷ a
❸ c
❹ c
❺ a
❻ b

16p
❶ b
❷❸ c
❹❻ a
❺ b

22p

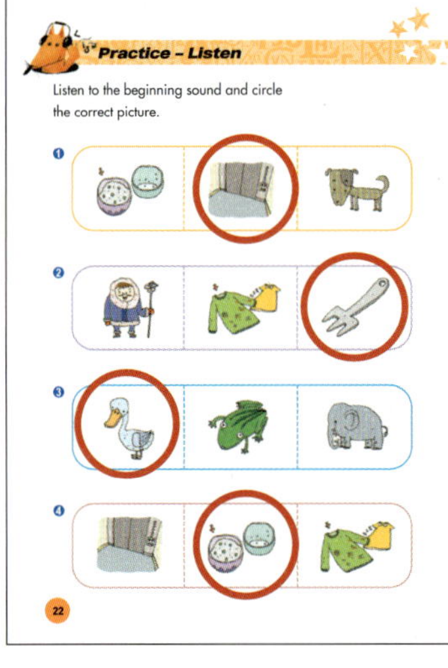

23p

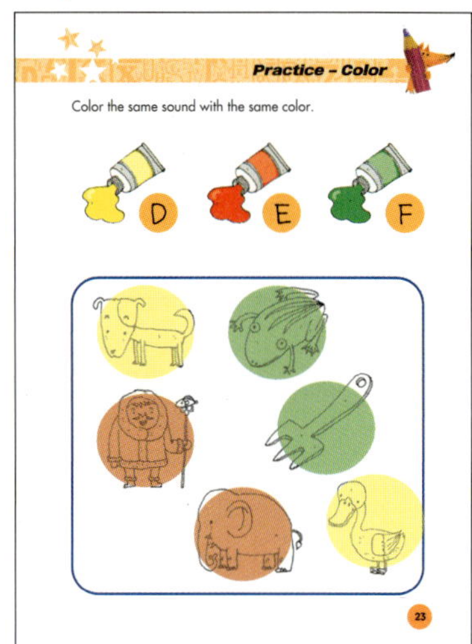

24p

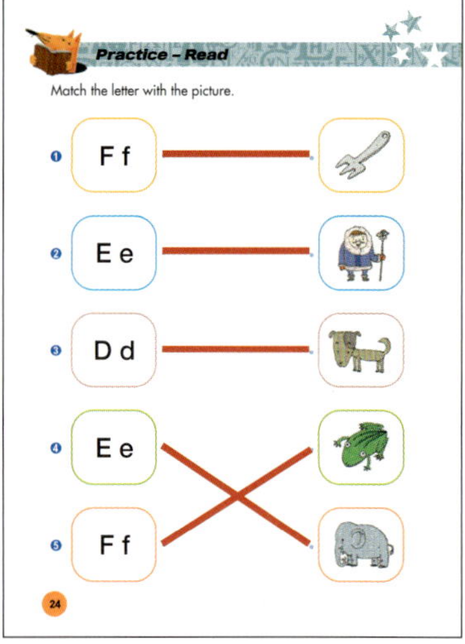

25p
❶ f
❷ d
❸ E
❹ d
❺ f

26p

❶ f
❷ d
❸ f
❹ ❻ E/e
❺ d

32p

❶ h
❷ g
❸ i
❹ l
❺ h
❻ g
❼ h
❽ g
❾ i

33p

34p

❶ Gg
❷ Ii
❸ Hh
❹ Ii
❺ Gg
❻ Hh

35p

❶ H
❷ I
❸ g
❹ h
❺ H
❻ G
❼ i
❽ g

36p

❶ g
❷ i
❸ ❹ h
❺ I
❻ g

Review1

38p

39p

❶ H　❷ c
❸ a　❹ G
❺ B　❻ d

40p

❶ F　❷ i
❸ C　❹ d
❺ H

41p

❶ c　❷ d
❸ g　❹ h
❺ e　❻ a

Answer Key

46p
1 l
2 k
3 j
4 k
5 j
6 l

47p

48p

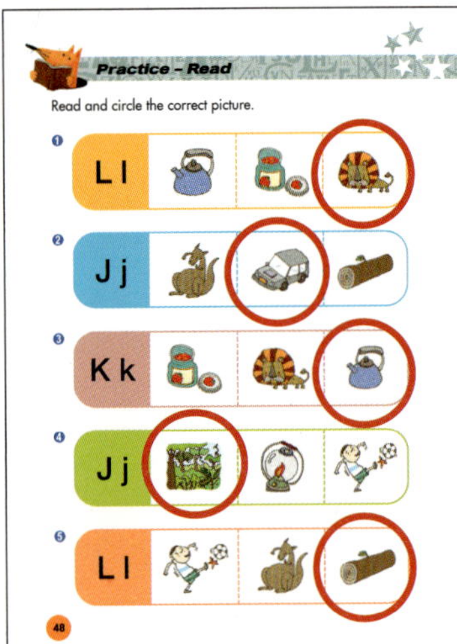

49p
1 j
2 k
3 l
4 k
5 j
6 l

50p
1 k
2 k
3 j
4 j
5 **6** l

56p

57p

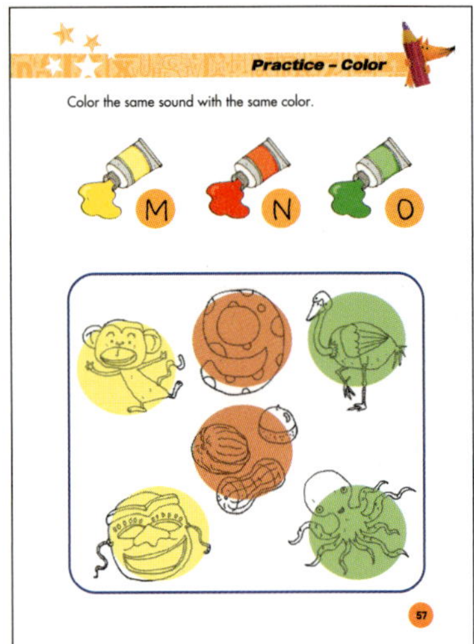

58p
1 nut
2 octopus
3 monkey
4 nine
5 omelet

59p
1 o
2 m
3 n
4 n
5 m

60p
1 n
2 **4** m
3 o
5 o
6 n

66p

❶ p
❷ r
❸ r
❹ q
❺ p
❻ q
❼ r
❽ q
❾ p

67p

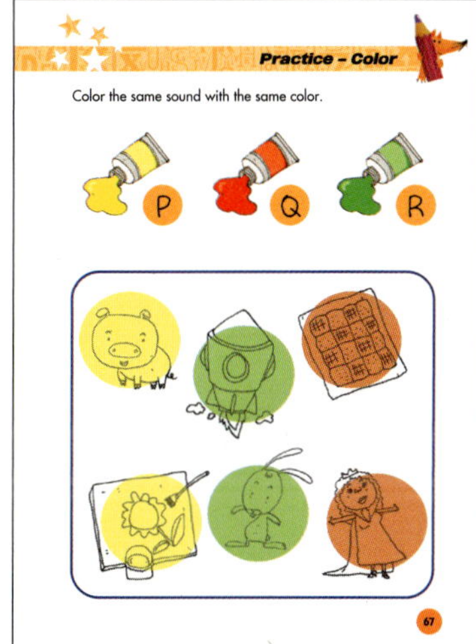

68p

❶ Qq
❷ Rr
❸ Pp
❹ Qq
❺ Rr
❻ Pp

69p

❶ R
❷ Q
❸ p
❹ q
❺ P
❻ R
❼ q
❽ r

70p

❶ r
❷ p
❸ r
❹ ❻ q
❺ p

Review2

72p

73p

❶ m　❷ o
❸ J　❹ q
❺ N　❻ R

74p

Answer Key

75p

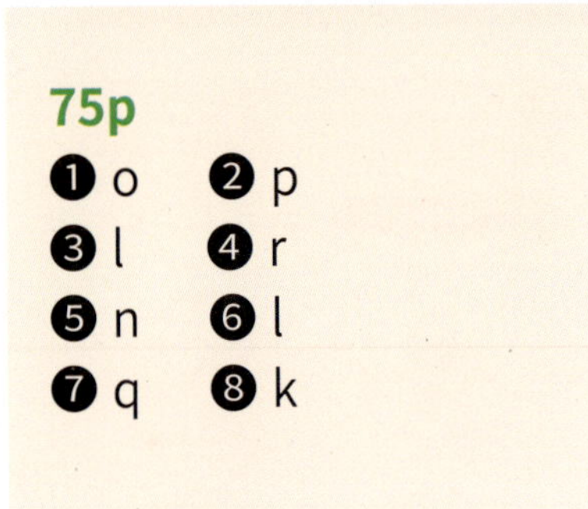

1. o 2. p
3. l 4. r
5. n 6. l
7. q 8. k

80p

1. t
2. s
3. u
4. u
5. s
6. t

81p

82p

83p

1. t
2. u
3. s
4. s
5. u
6. t

84p

1. t
2. s
3. s
4. 6. u
5. s

90p

91p

92p

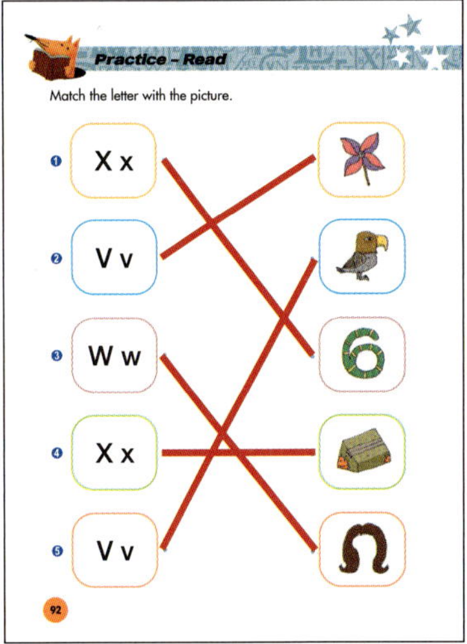

101p

Review2

106p

107p

93p

❶ v
❷ w
❸ w
❹ x
❺ v

94p

❶ v
❷ x
❸ ❹ w
❺ v
❻ x

100p

❶ z
❷ y
❸ y
❹ z
❺ z
❻ y

102p

❶ Zz
❷ Yy
❸ Zz
❹ Yy
❺ Yy
❻ Zz

103p

❶ Y
❷ Z
❸ z
❹ z
❺ Y
❻ y

104p

❶ ❹ z
❷ y
❸ ❻ y
❺ z

108p

❶ u ❷ w
❸ y ❹ x
❺ s ❻ v
❼ t ❽ z

121

109p

❶ x ❷ w
❸ x ❹ t
❺ y ❻ y
❼ w ❽ t

Test

110p

❶ Kk
❷ Ff
❸ Zz
❹ Pp
❺ Ee

111p

❶ F
❷ F
❸ T
❹ F
❺ F
❻ T
❼ T
❽ T

112p

113p

❶ seal
❷ nine
❸ horse
❹ quilt
❺ big

114p

❶ ⓐ
❷ ⓒ
❸ ⓑ
❹ ⓒ
❺ ⓑ

115p

❶ Aa
❷ Oo
❸ Kk
❹ Ii
❺ Cc
❻ Ll
❼ Ff
❽ Pp

123

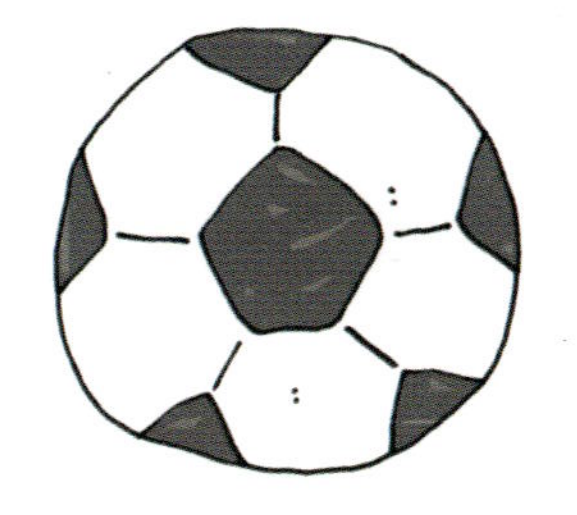

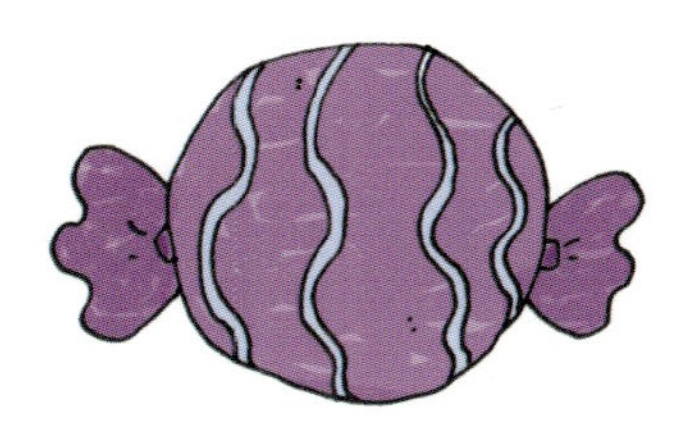

Eskimo	**c**andy	**b**ig	**a**nt
elephant	**d**irty	**b**all	**a**pple
elevator	**d**og	**c**at	**a**nimal
fork	**d**uck	**c**rown	**b**ear

frog	full	gorilla	guitar
garden	hen	horse	hill
Indian	iguana	insect	jeep
jungle	jam	kangaroo	kick

kettle

lion

lamp

log

monkey

make

mask

nine

nut

net

octopus

omelet

ostrich

pink

pig

paint

quail

queen

quilt

rocket

rabbit

rose

seal

sing

sea

twins

tiger

tree

ugly

uncle

umbrella

vulture

vane

vest

wolf

wet

wig

six

fox

box

yak

yell

yawn

zoo

zero

zebra

JUMP UP Phonics

개정판 **1**

initial Sounds ★ Workbook

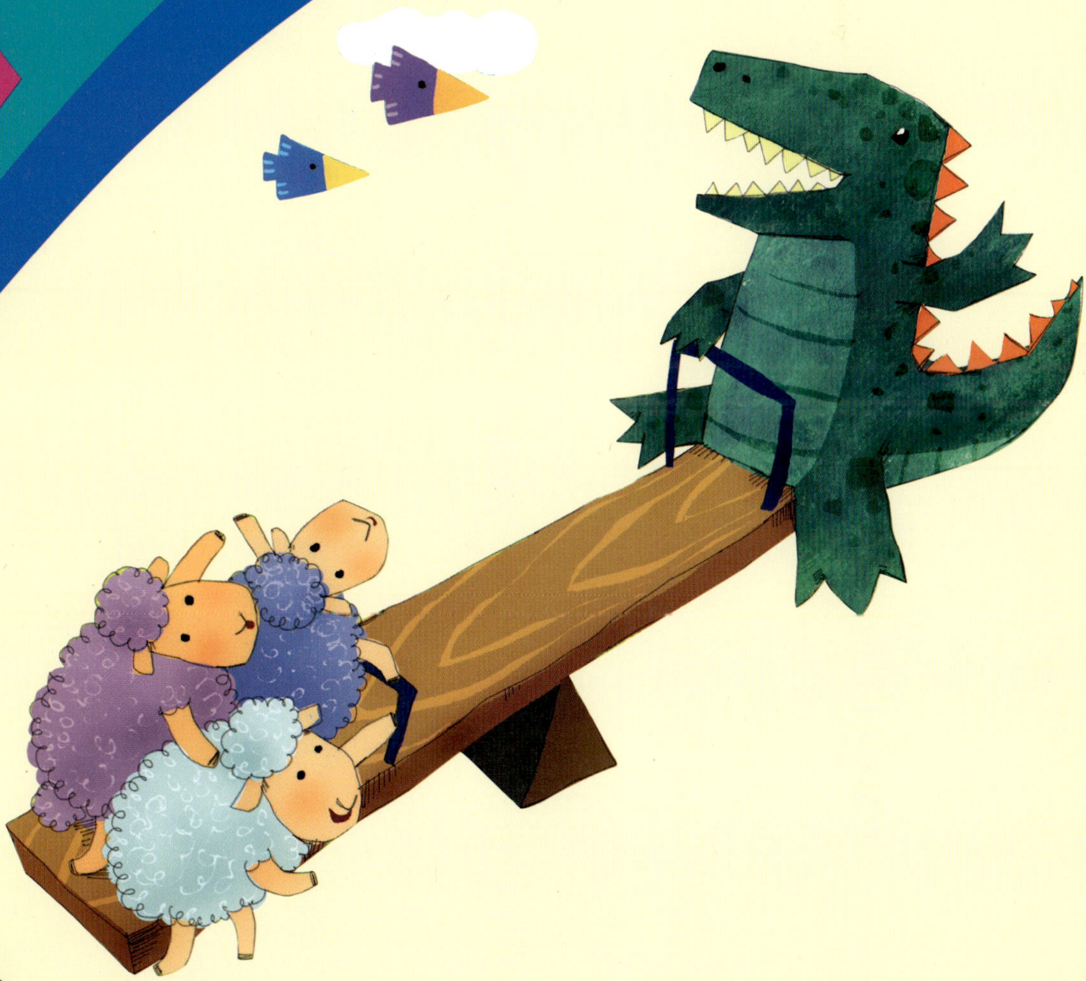

International Linguistics Research Institute

CONTENTS

A Look and Write.

ant

apple

animal

bear

big

ball

cat

crown

candy

 Circle the correct picture.

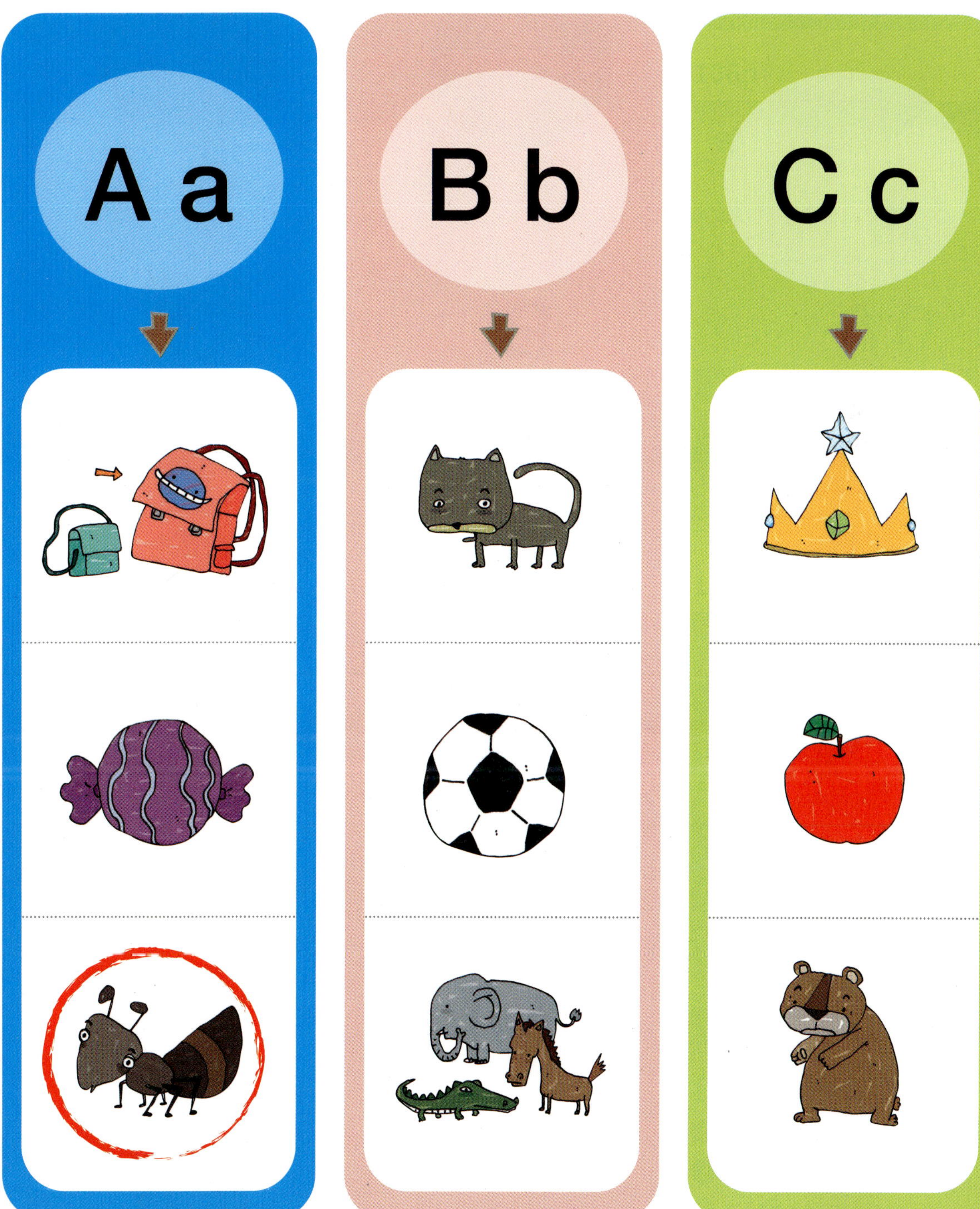

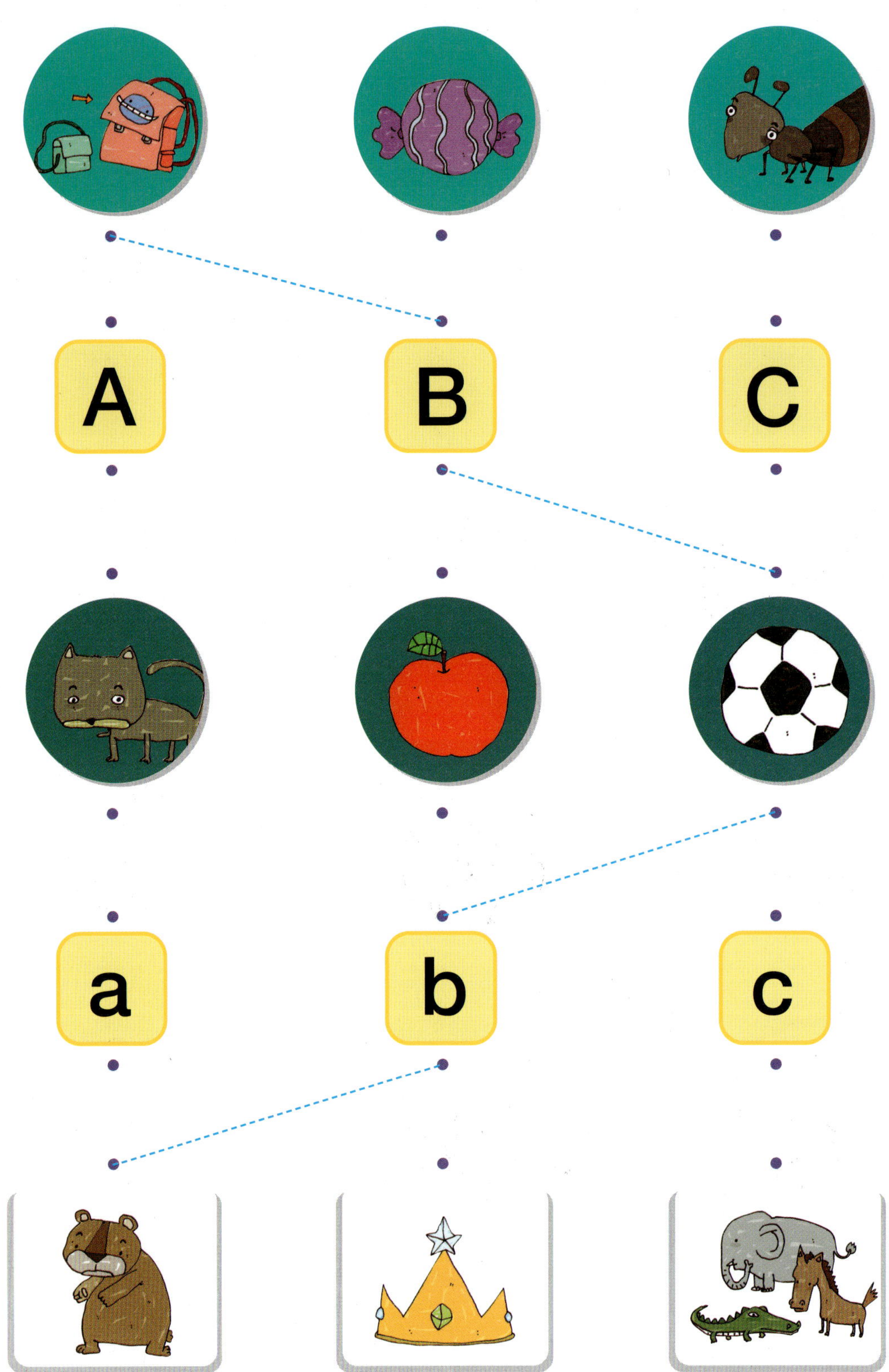

A
B
C
a
b
c

D Circle the correct letter.

a
b
(c)

a
b
c

a
b
c

E Match and Color.

A a   B b   C c

Trace and Write.

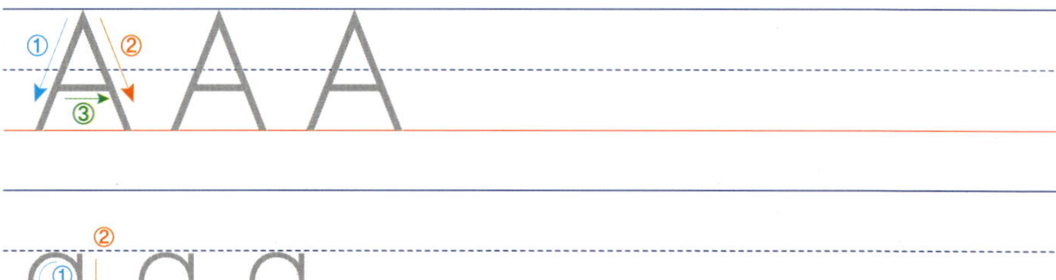

ant

ball

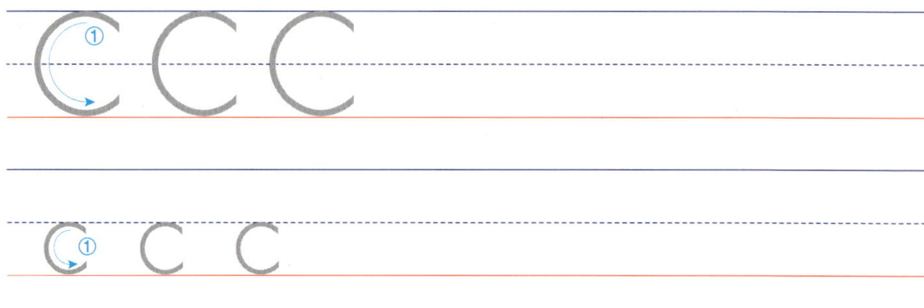

crown

A Look and Write.

dirty

dog

duck

Eskimo

elephant

elevator

fork

frog

full

 Circle the correct picture.

C Look and Connect.

D

E

F

d

e

f

D Circle the correct letter.

d
e
f

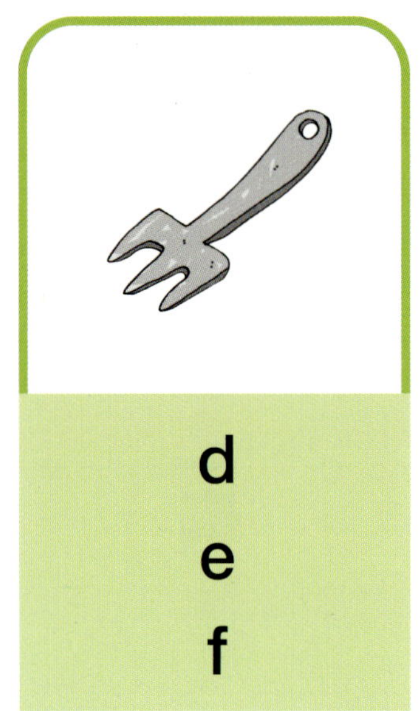

d
e
f

d
e
f

E Match and Color.

D d

E e

F f

dog

elevator

fork

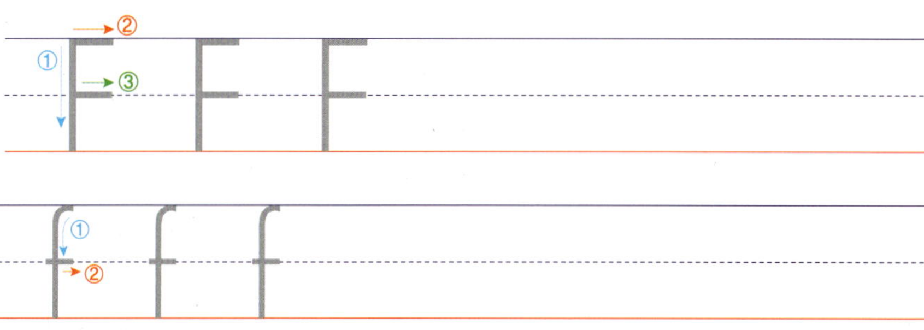

A Look and Write.

gorilla

guitar

garden

hen

horse

hill

indian

iguana

insect

B Circle the correct picture.

G g

H h

I i

 Look and Connect.

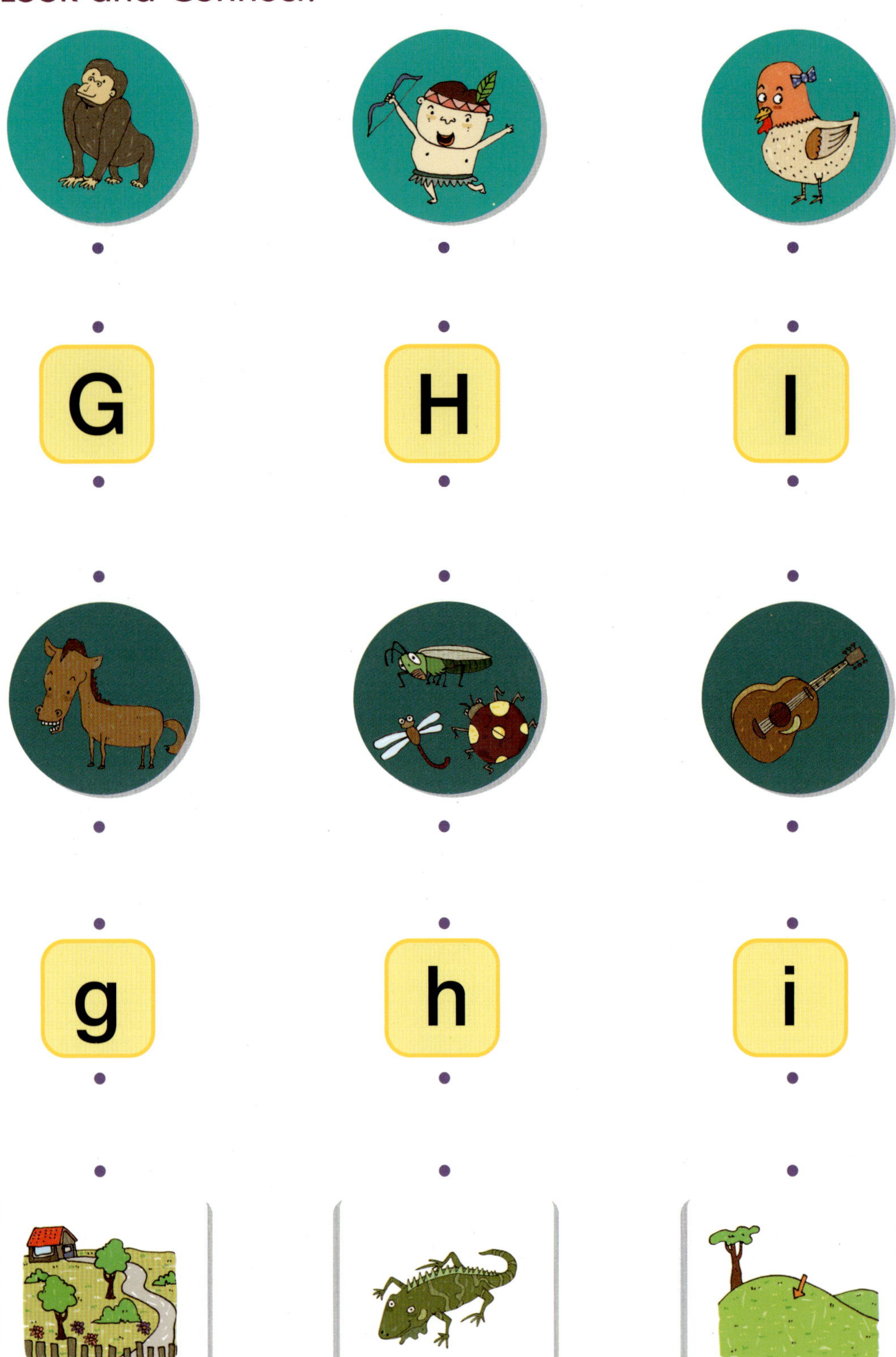

g
h
i

g
h
i

g
h
i

E Match and Color.

G g

H h

I i

gorilla

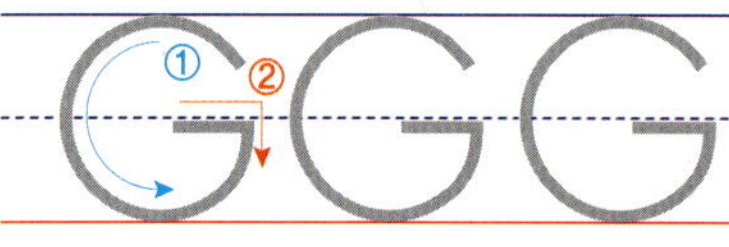

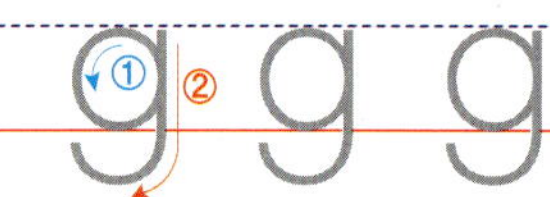

hen

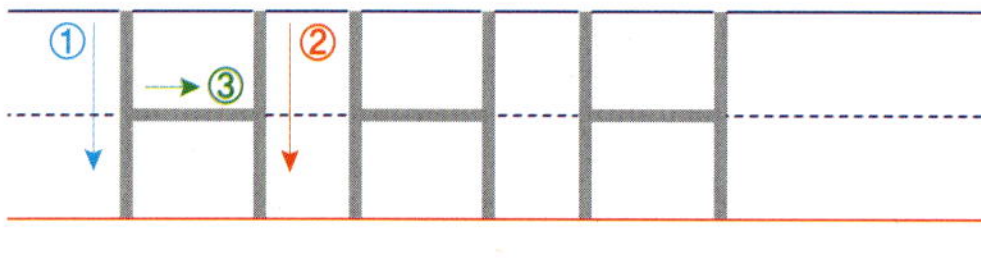

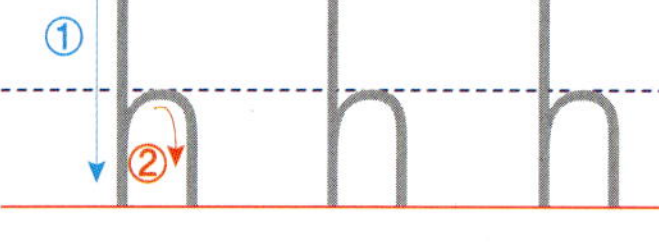

iguana

A Write the partner letters.

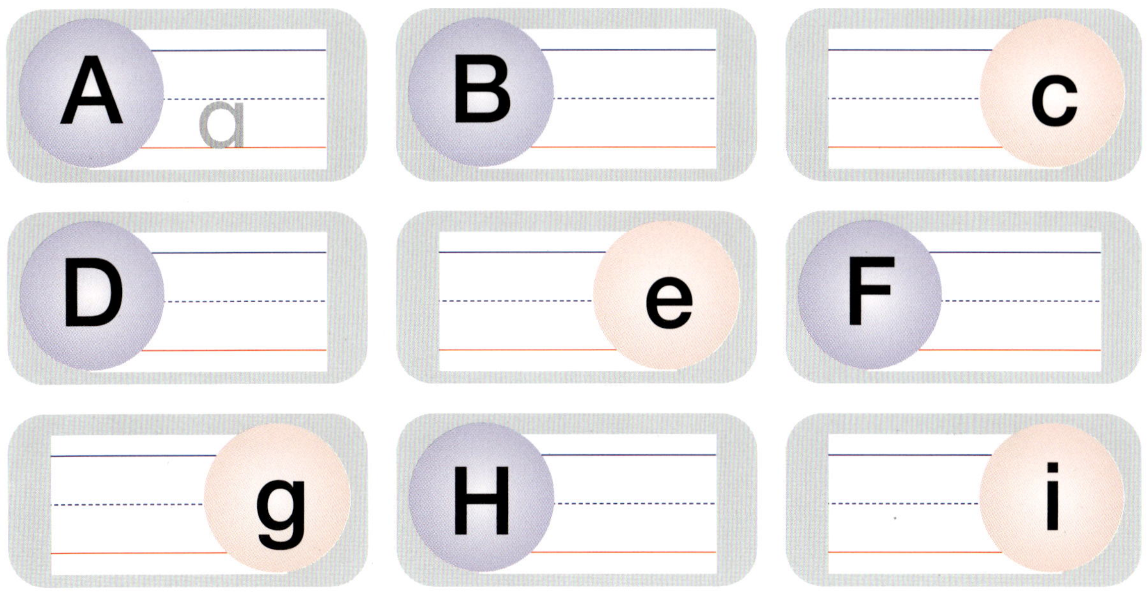

B Look and Match.

B   D   F   H

C Circle the beginning letter.

D Check the correct picture.

E Match the same beginning sounds.

   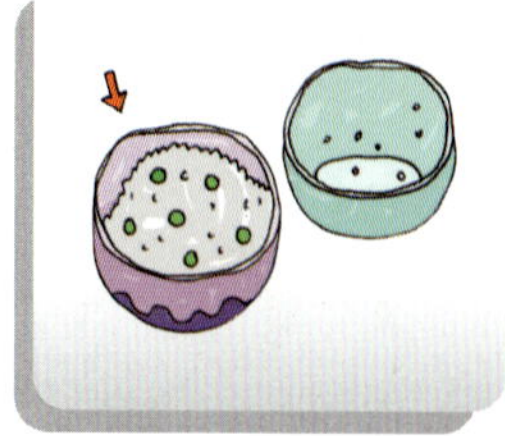

  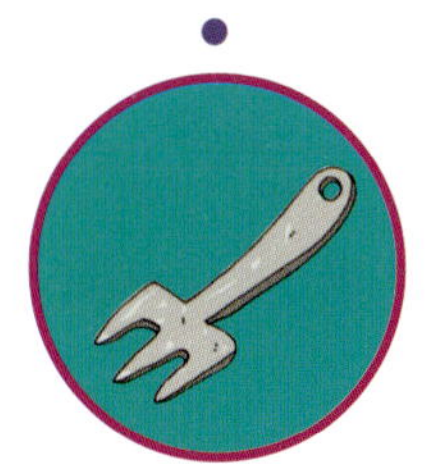 

F Read and Match.

Eskimo   animal   Indian   cat

Look and Write the beginning letters.

Unit 4   J j K k L l

A Look and Write.

jeep

jungle

jam

kangaroo

kick

kettle

lion

lamp

log

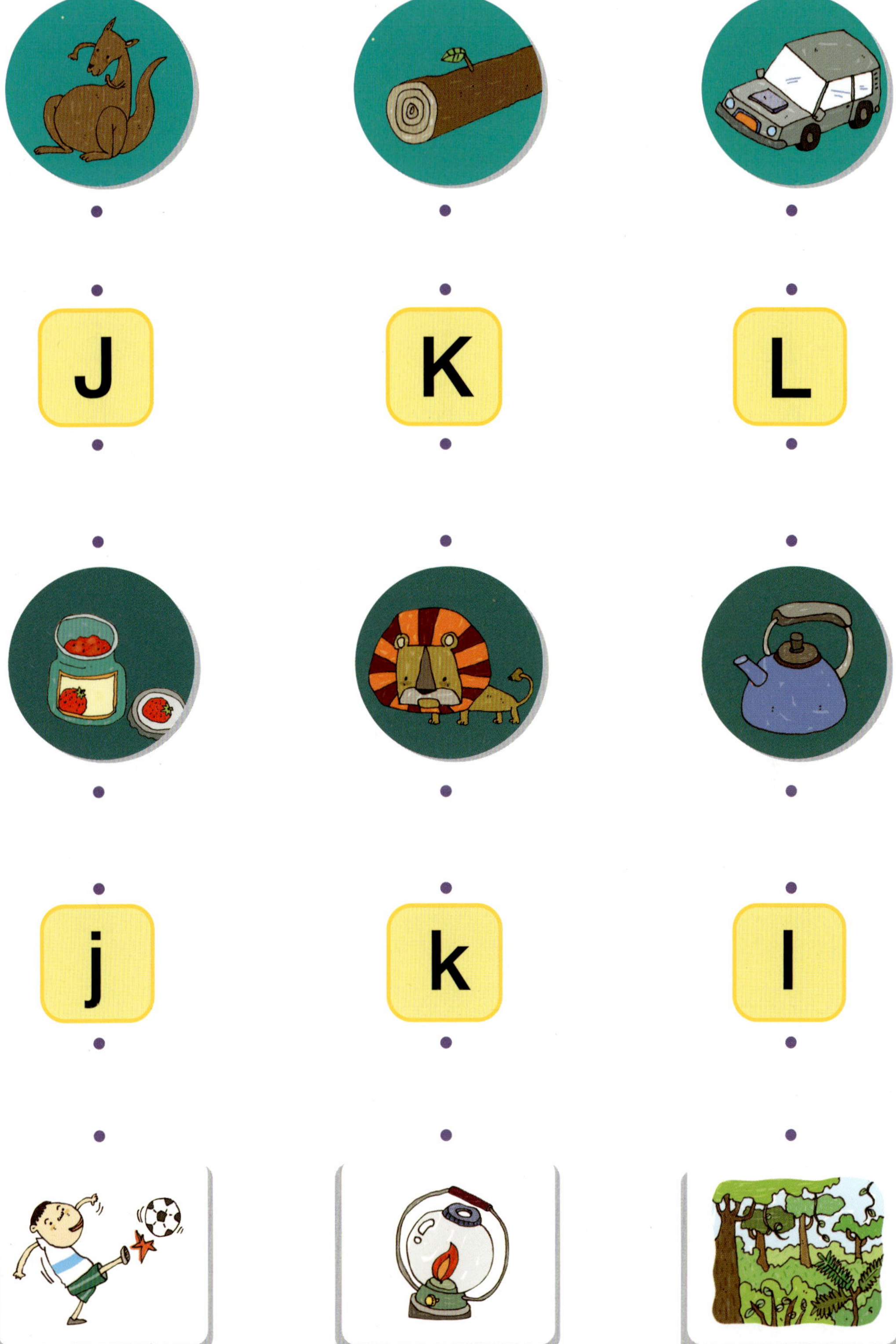

J
K
L
j
k
l

D Circle the correct letter.

j
k
l

j
k
l

j
k
l

E Match and Color.

jam

kick

lamp

A Look and Write.

 monkey

 make

 mask

 nine

 nut

 net

 octopus

 omelet

 ostrich

M m

N n

O o

 Look and Connect.

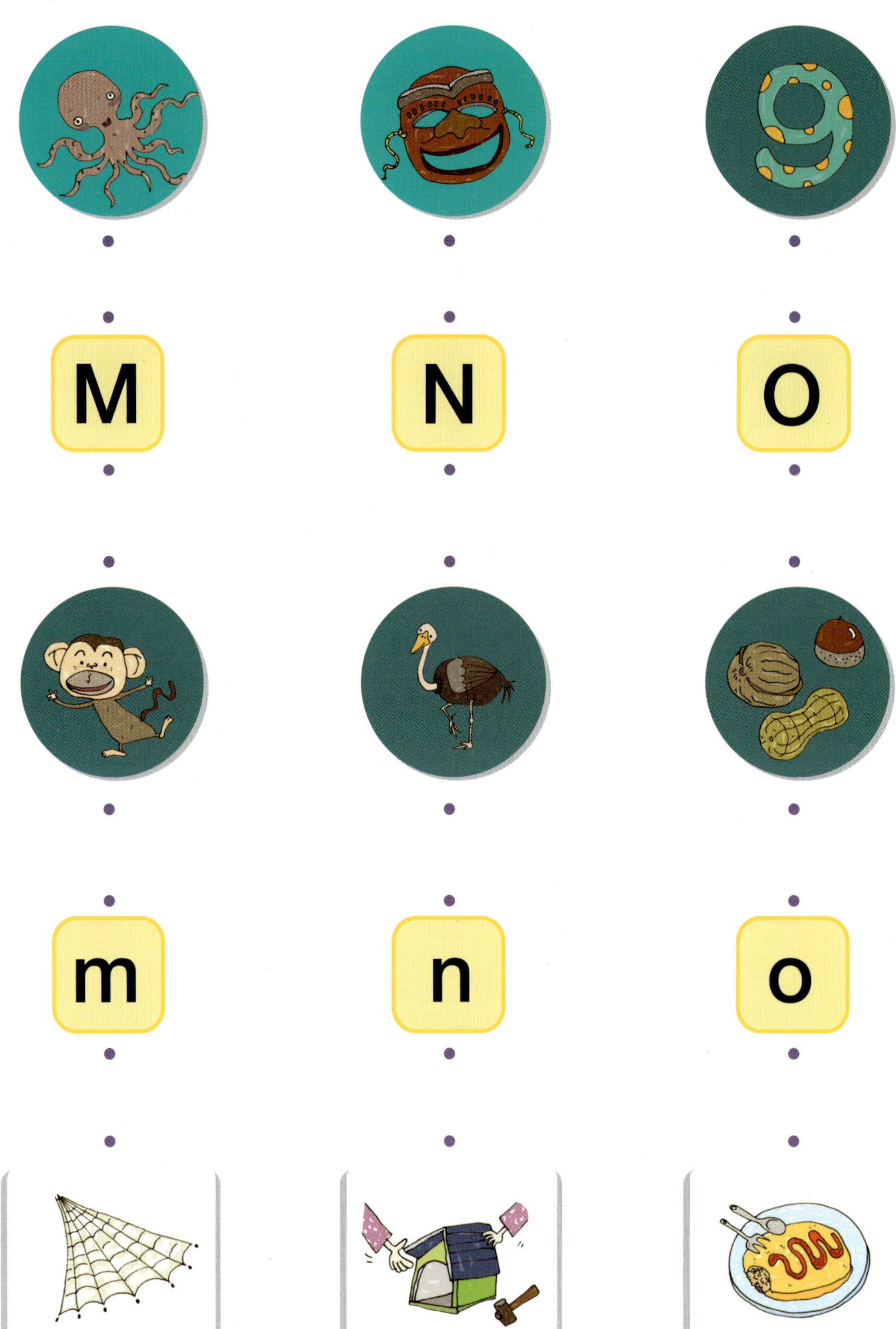

D Circle the correct letter.

m
n
o

m
n
o

m
n
o

E Match and Color.

mask

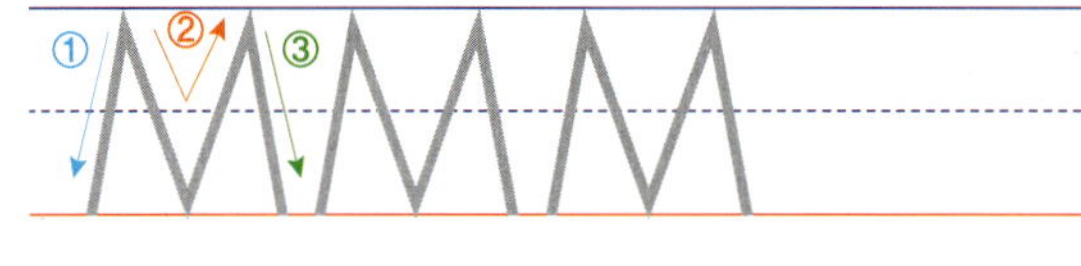

nut

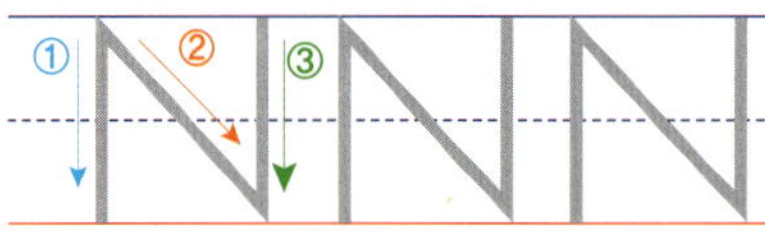

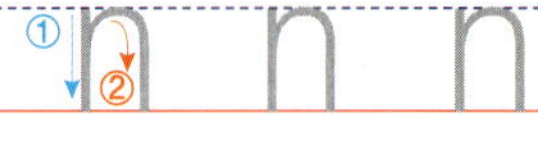

ostrich

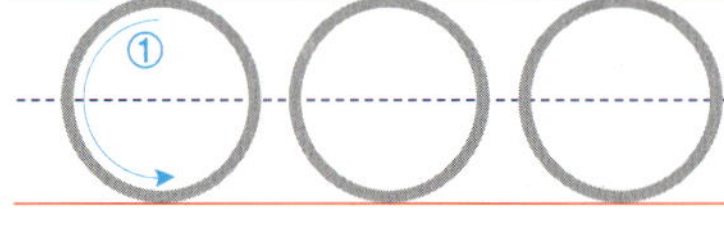

A Look and Write.

paint

pig

pink

quail

queen

quilt

rocket

rabbit

rose

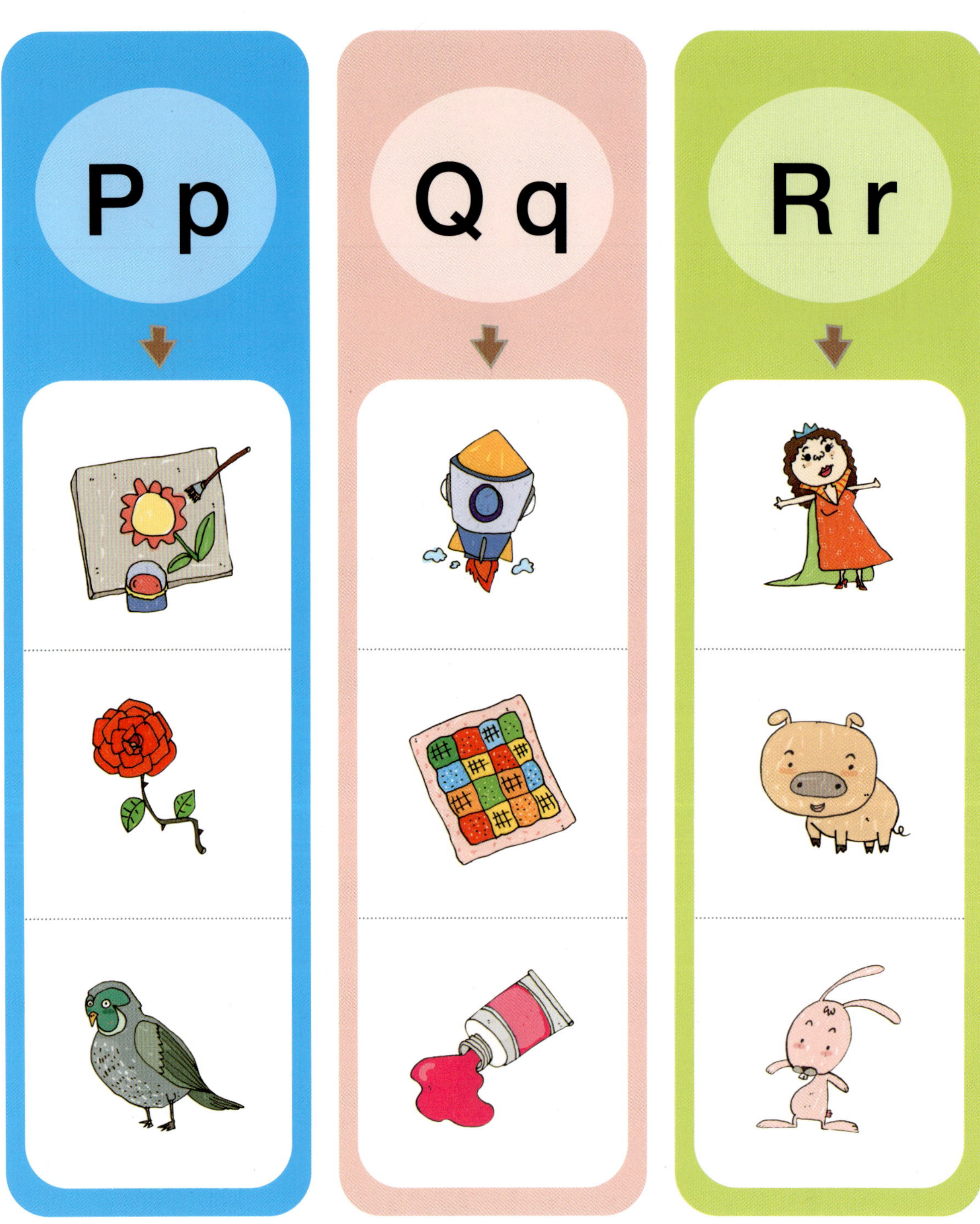

P p
Q q
R r

C Look and Connect.

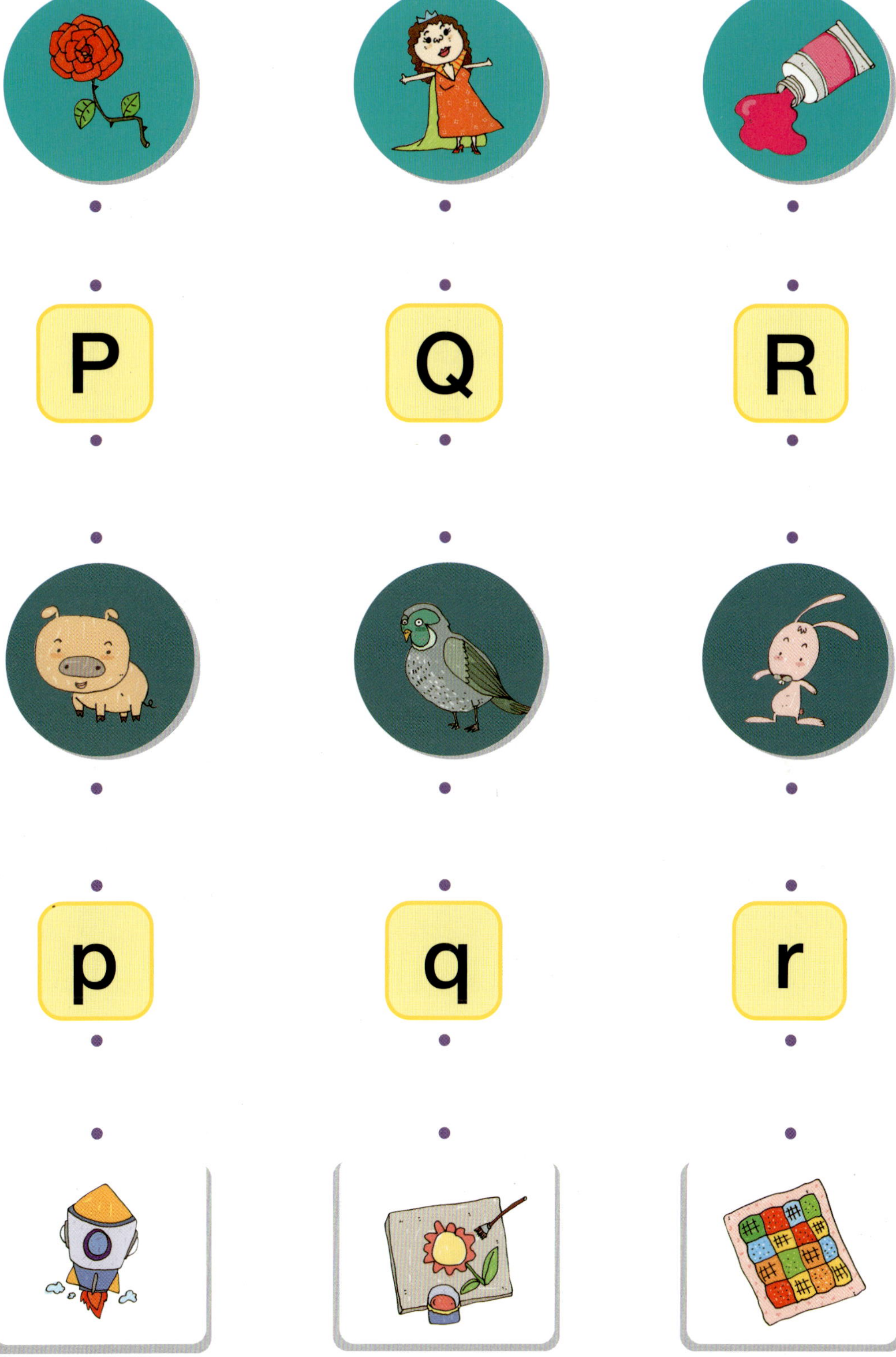

 Circle the correct letter.

p
q
r

p
q
r

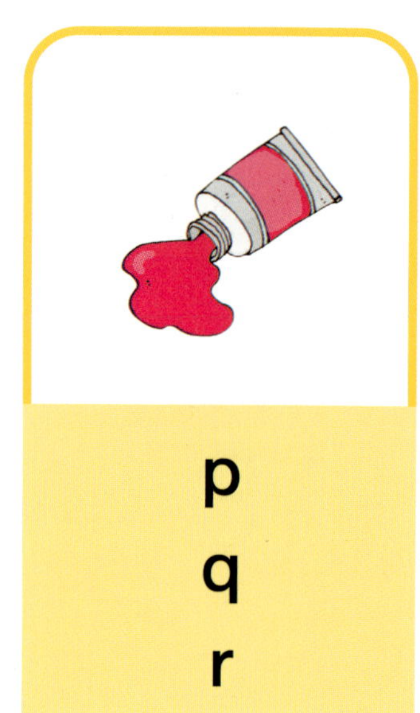

p
q
r

E Match and Color.

pink
quail
rabbit

A Write the partner letters.

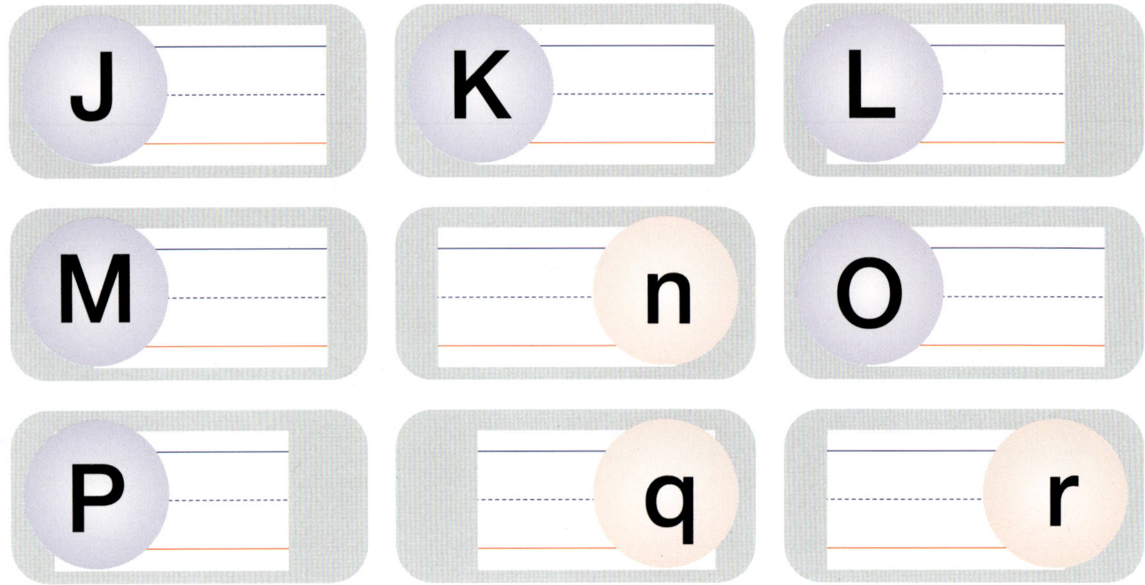

J   K   L

M   n   O

P   q   r

B Look and Match.

K   M   O   P

  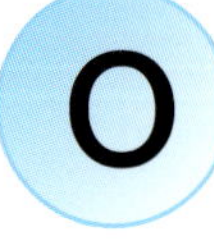 

D Check the correct picture.

 Match the same beginning sounds.

F **Read and Match.**

jeep   rabbit   nut   lion

Look and Write the beginning letters.

A Look and Write.

seal

sing

sea

twins

tiger

tree

ugly

uncle

umbrella

Circle the correct picture.

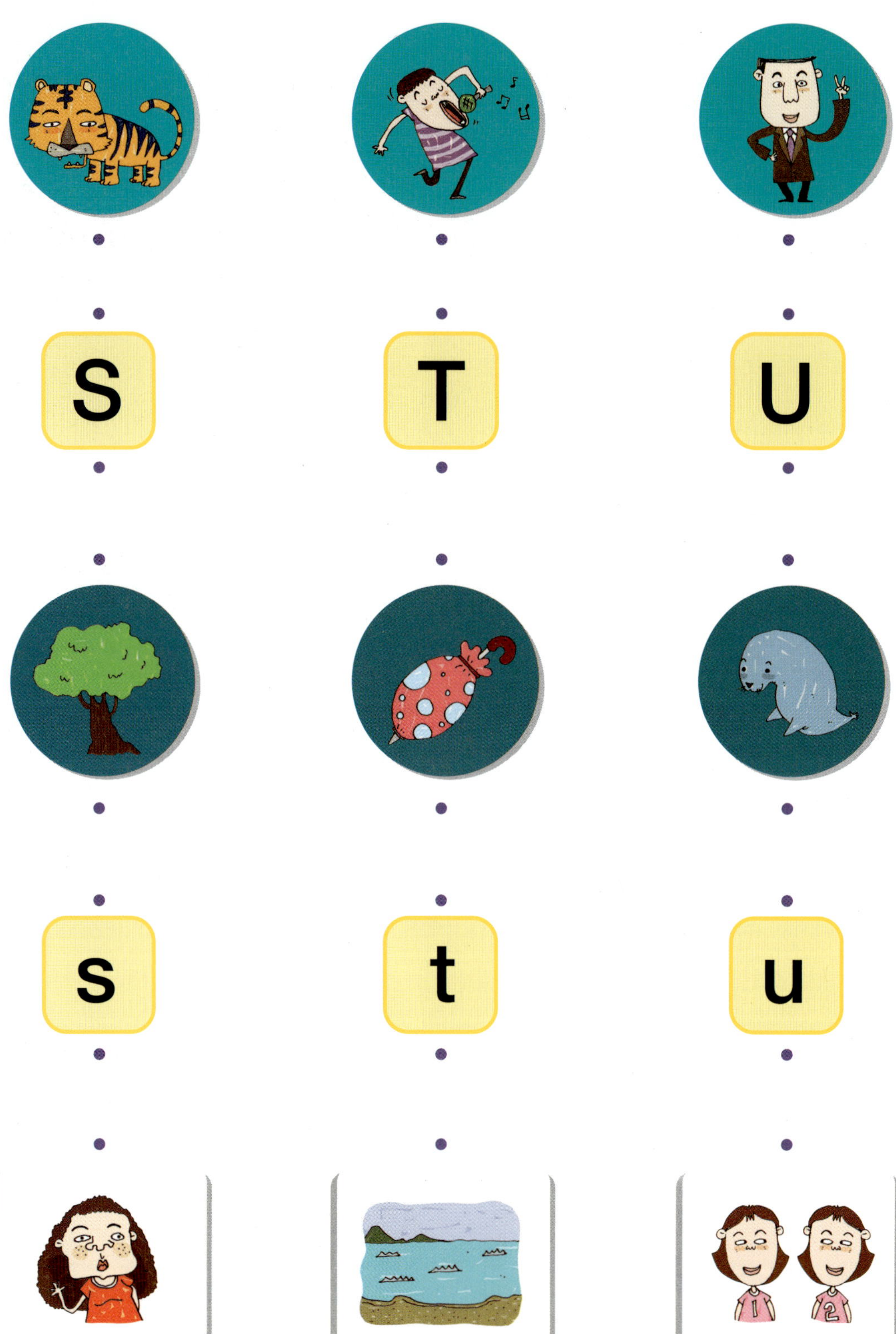

S

T

U

s

t

u

 Circle the correct letter.

s
t
u

s
t
u

s
t
u

E **Match and Color.**

 Trace and Write.

sing

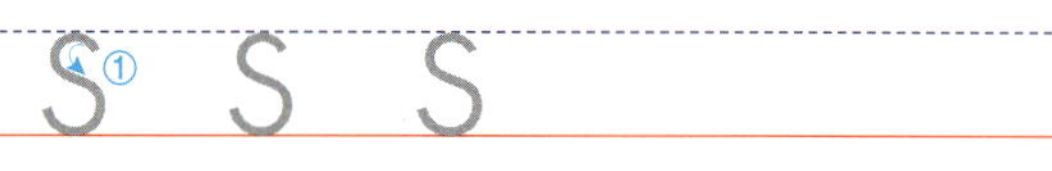

S S S

S S S

tiger

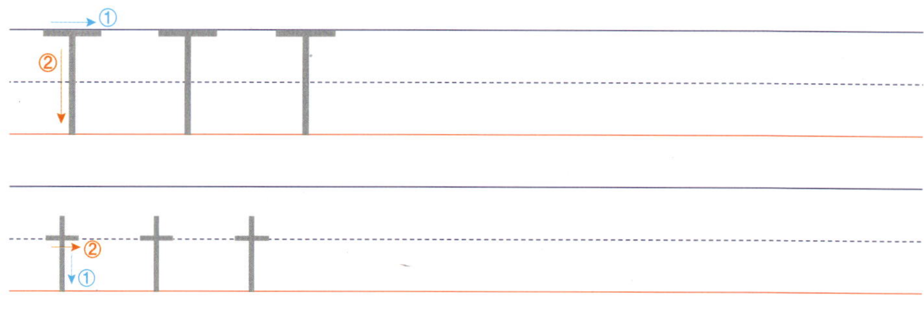

T T T T

T T T

uncle

U U U

U U U

Unit 8 Vv Ww Xx

A Look and Write.

vulture

vane

vest

wolf

wet

wig

six

fox

box

 Look and Connect.

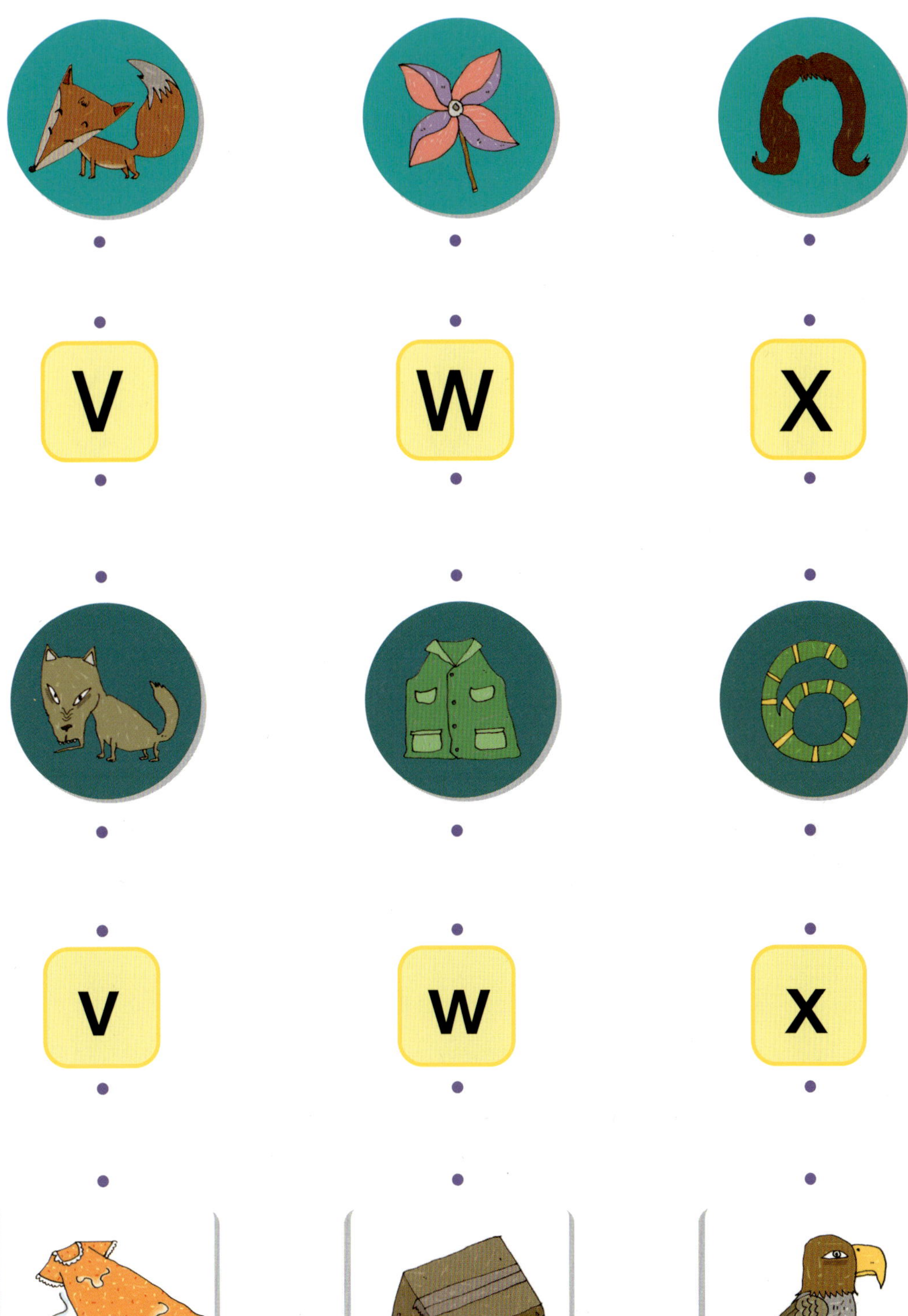

 Circle the correct letter.

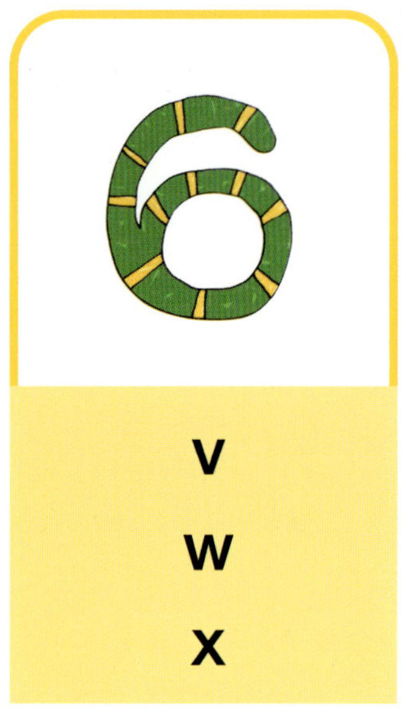

V
W
X

V
W
X

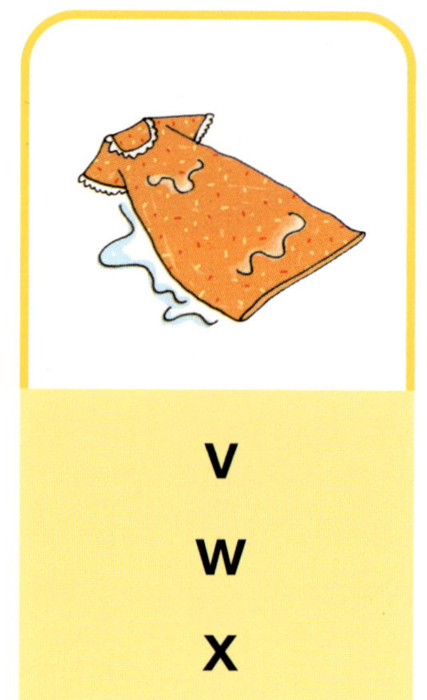

V
W
X

E Match and Color.

vest
wig
fox

A Look and Write.

yak

yell

yawn

zoo

zero

zebra

Y

y

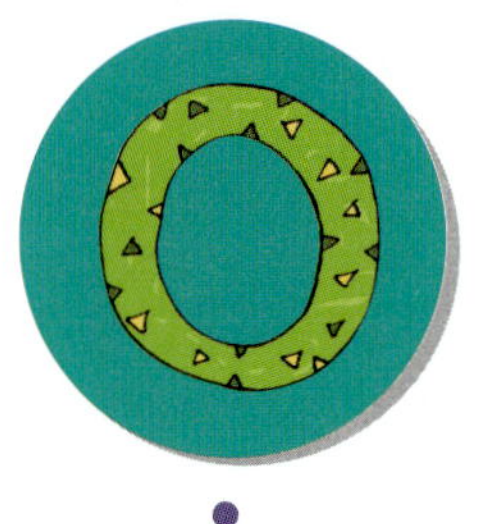

Z

z

D Circle the correct letter.

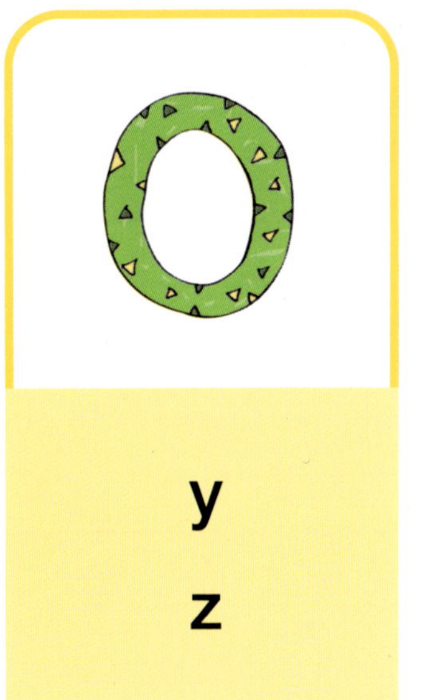

y

z

y

z

E Match and Color.

yell
zero

A Write the partner letters.

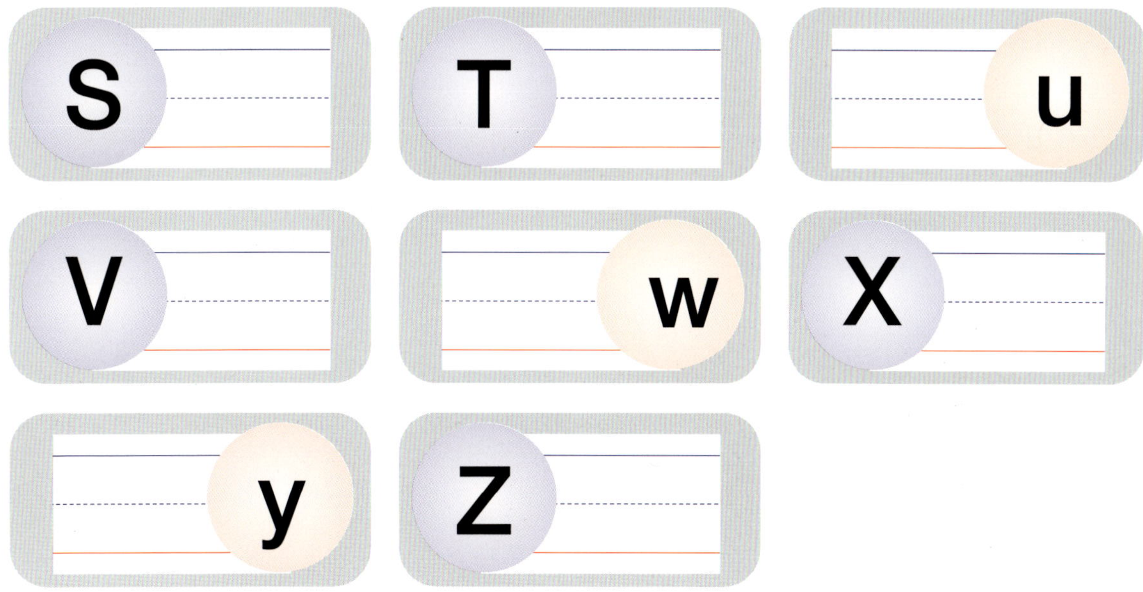

S	T	u
V	w	X
y	Z	

B Look and Match.

 z
 v
 w
 s

C Circle the beginning letter.

s t u
t u v
u v w
v w x
x y z
x y z

D Check the correct picture.

T t
U u
S s
Y y

 Match the same beginning sounds.

F Read and Match.

zoo	six	uncle	tree

Look and Write the beginning letters.

A Match the same beginning sounds and Write.

C Circle the beginning letter.

Bb Cc Dd

Aa Ee Gg

Ff Gg Hh

Gg Jj Zz

Ll Rr Yy

Ii Mm Nn

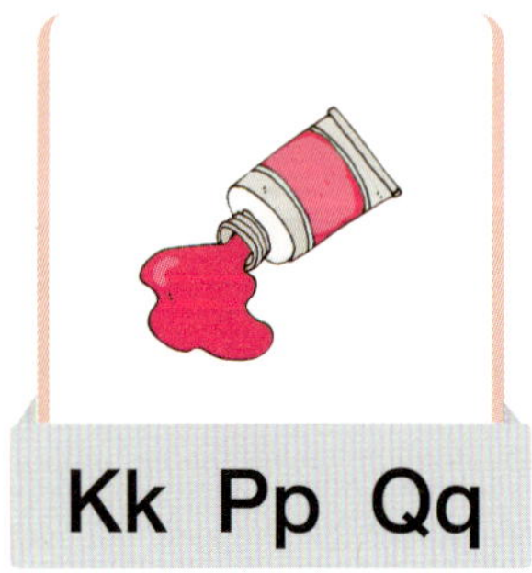

Kk Pp Qq

Ee Ll Rr

Tt Kk Xx

Aa Oo Uu

Bb Dd Vv

Gg Zz Rr

Color the right partner letters.

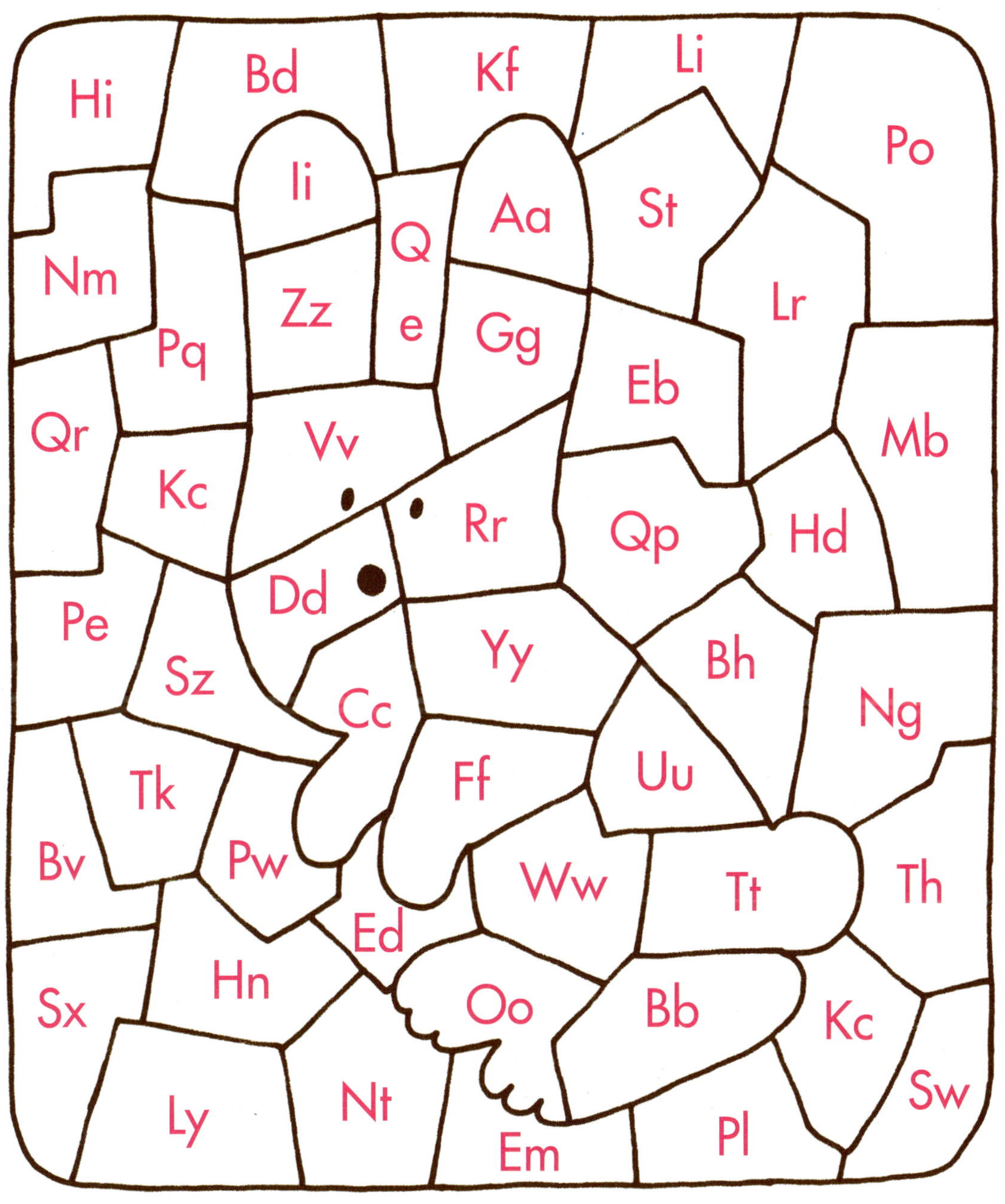

137p

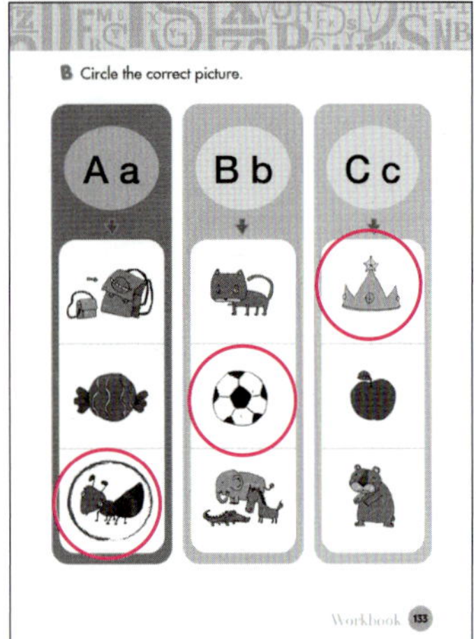

142p

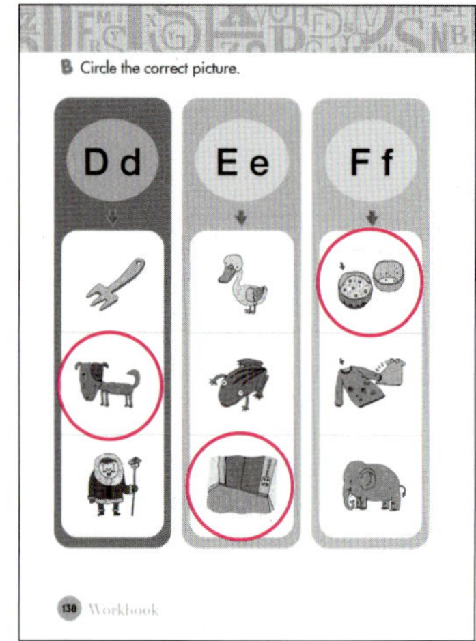

147p

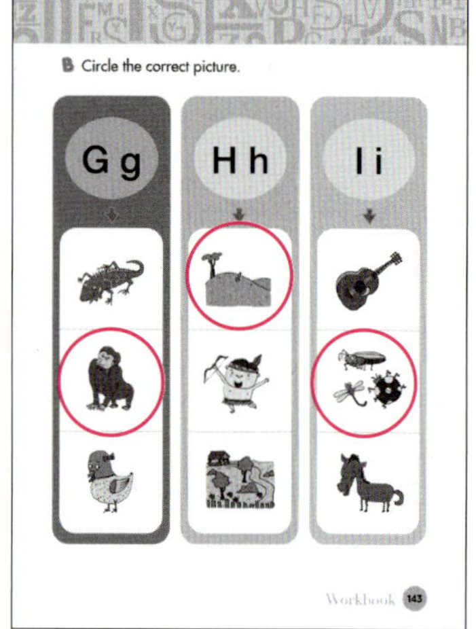

138p

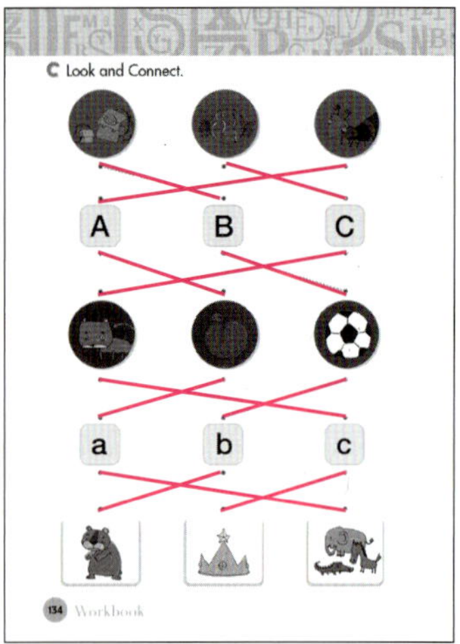

143p

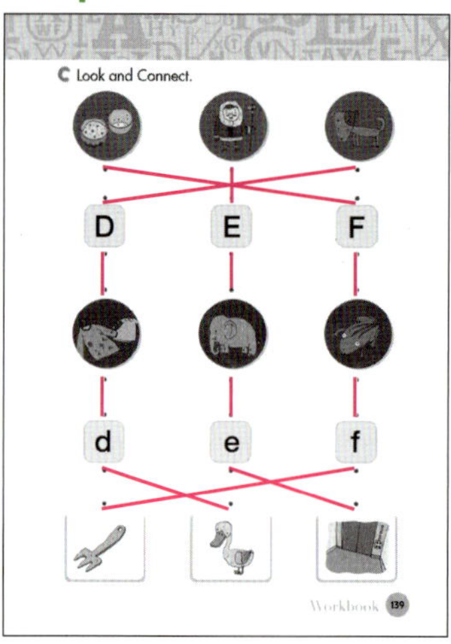

148p

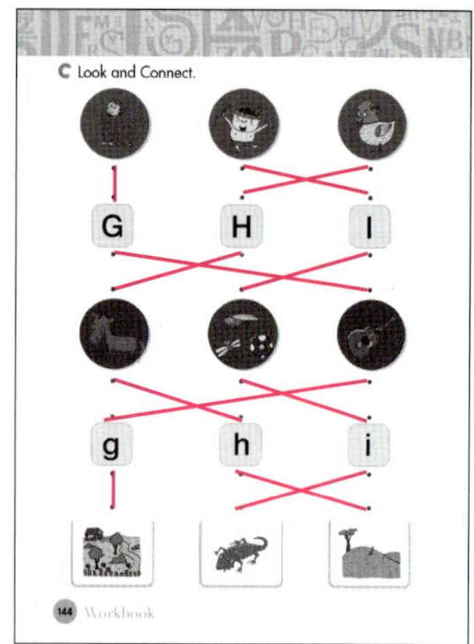

139p

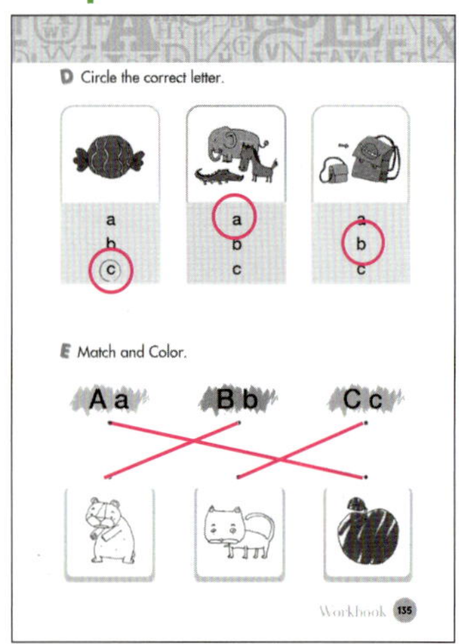

144p

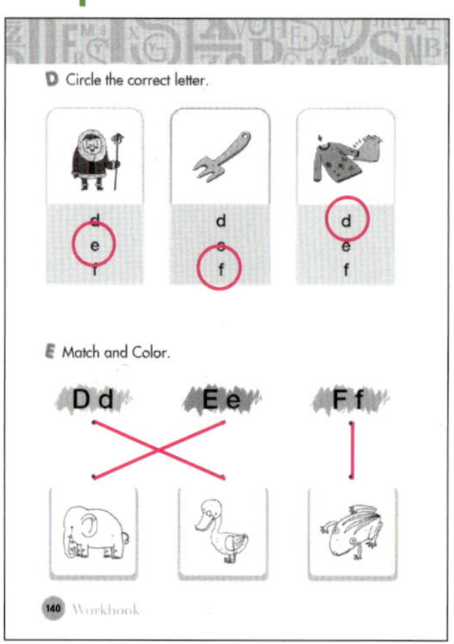

149p

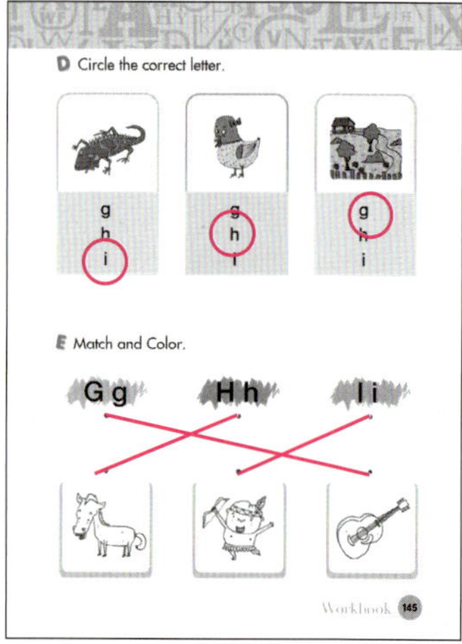

196 Workbook

151p

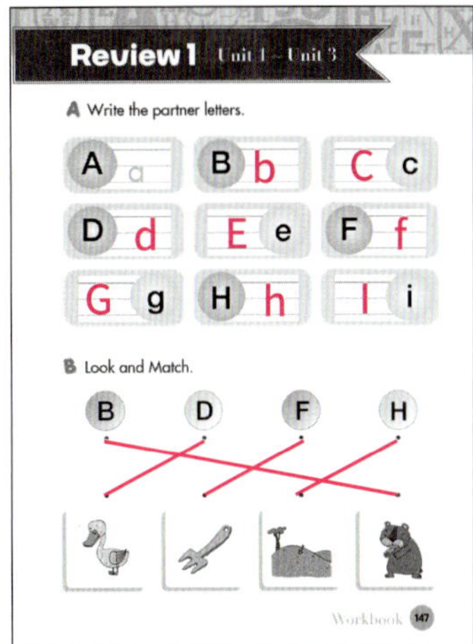

152p

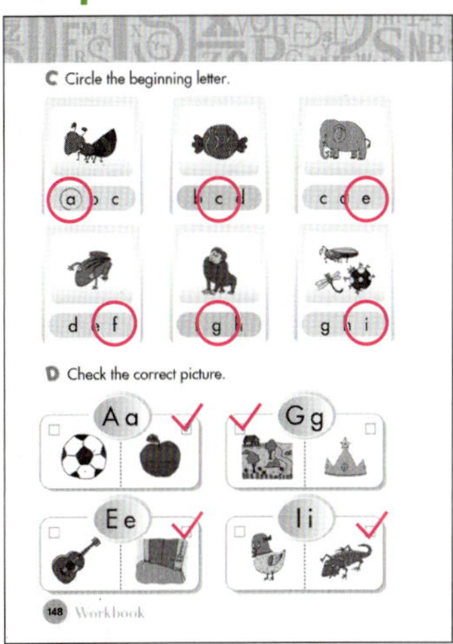

153p

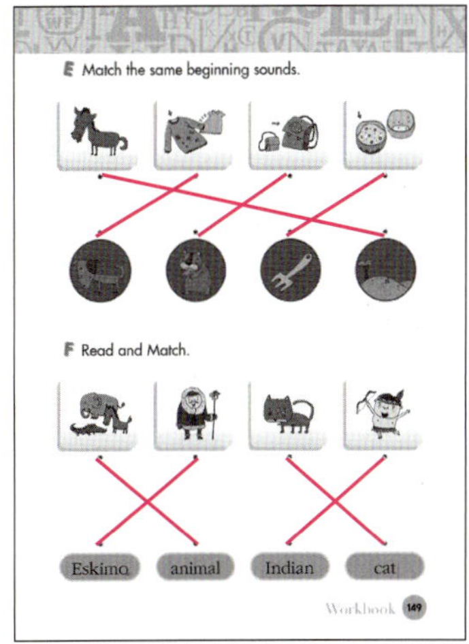

154p

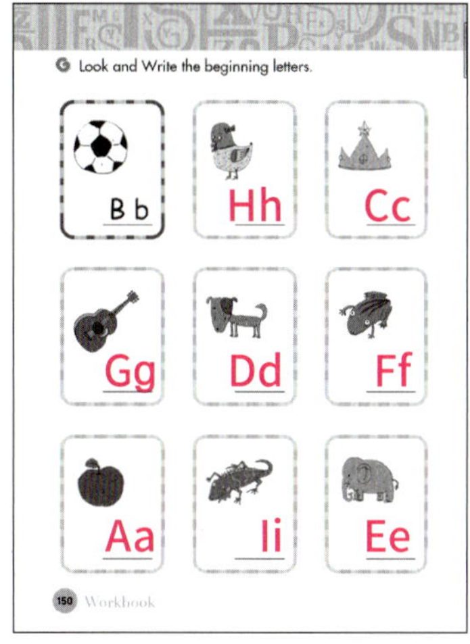

156p

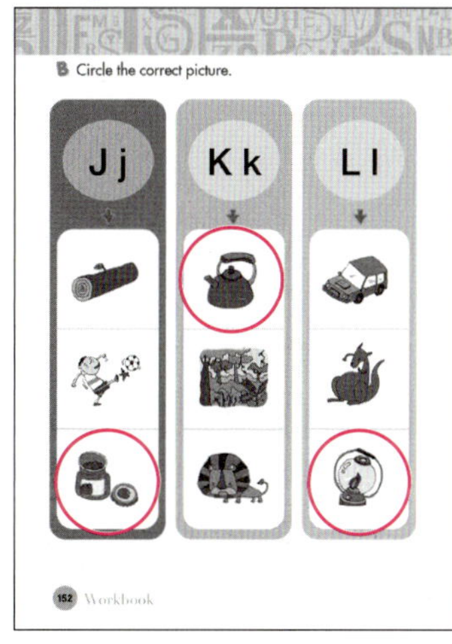

157p

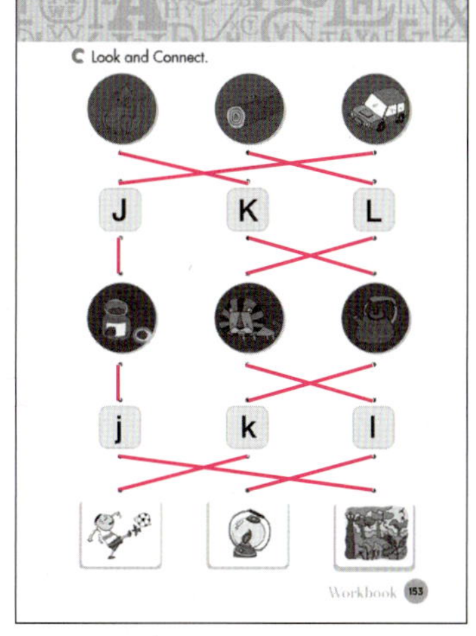

158p

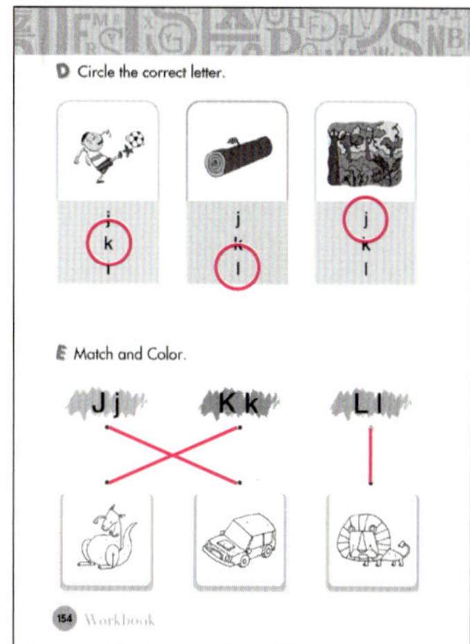

161p

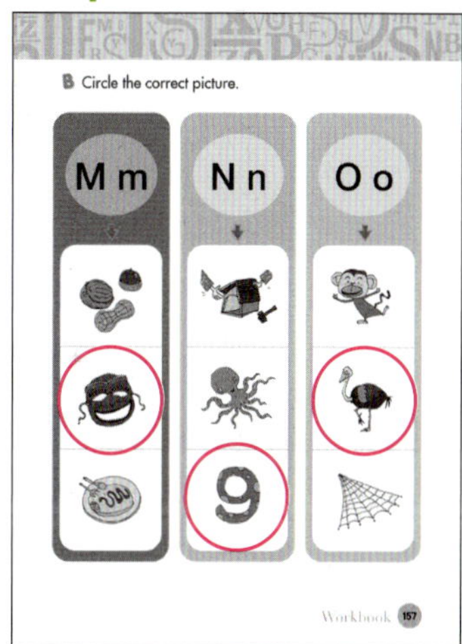

162p

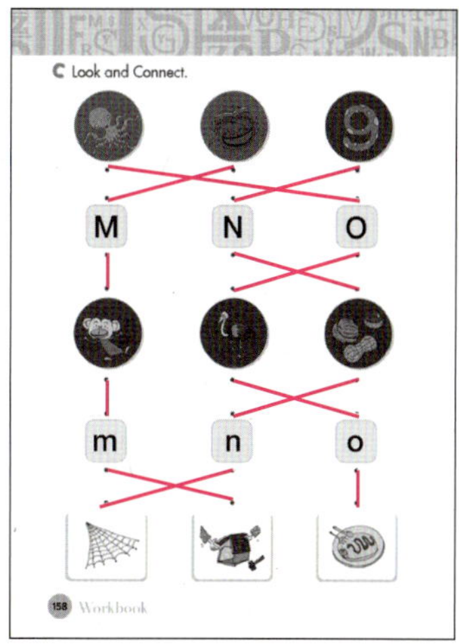

Answer Key

163p

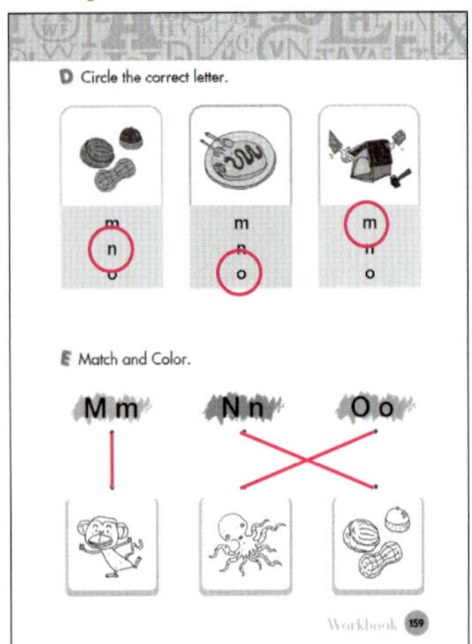

166p

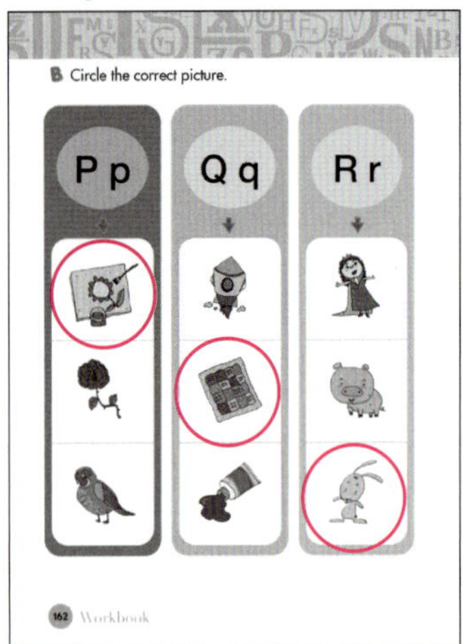

167p

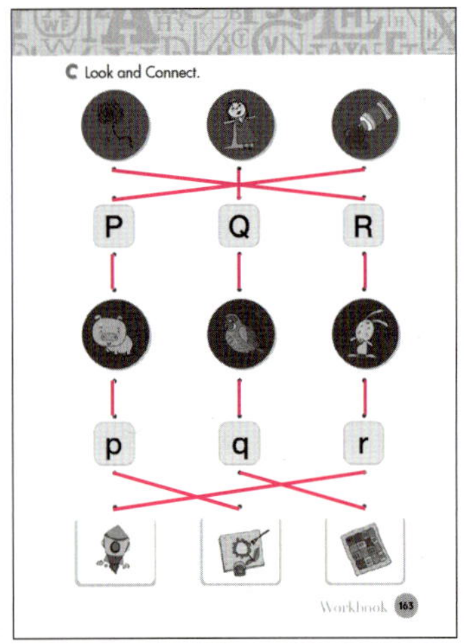

168p

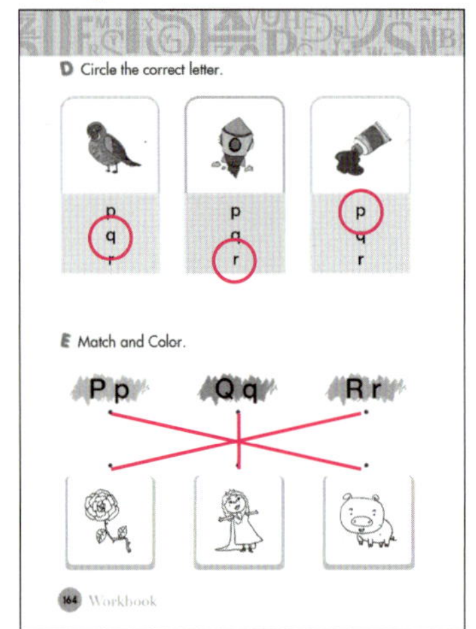

170p

171p

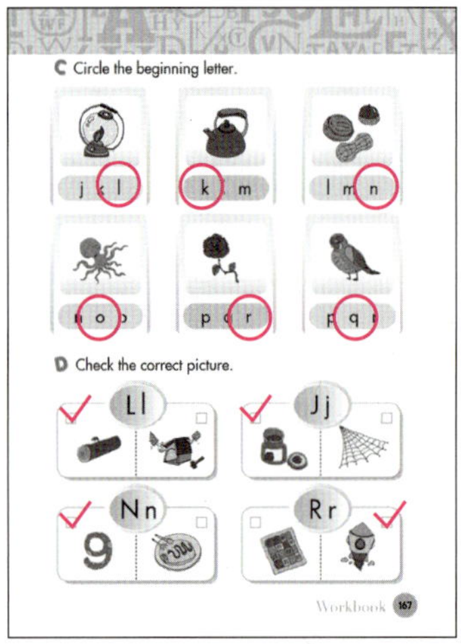

172p

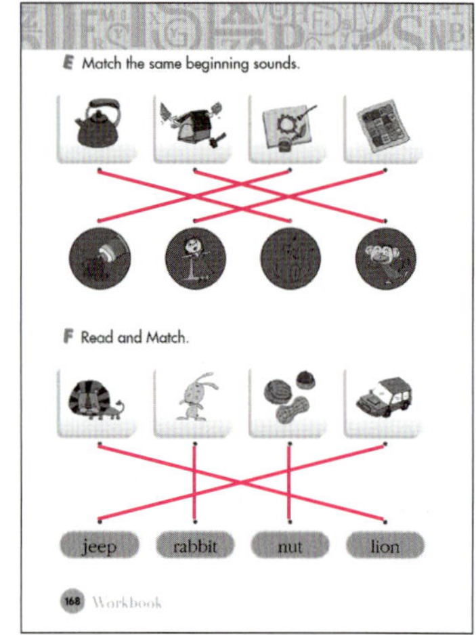

173p

175p

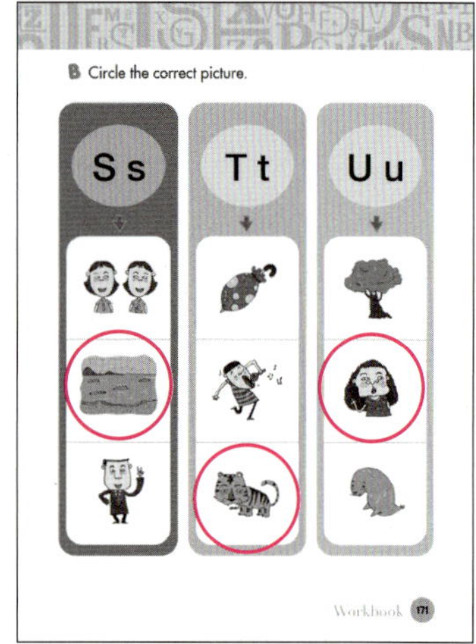

176p

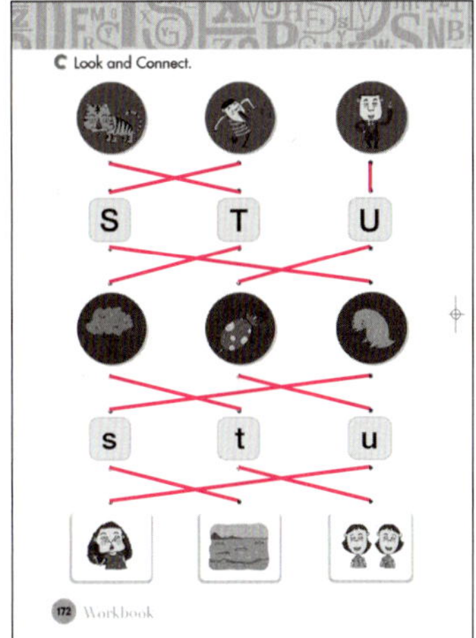

177p

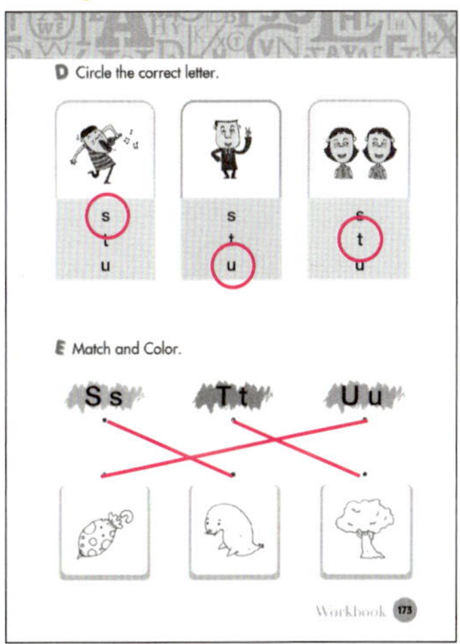

180p

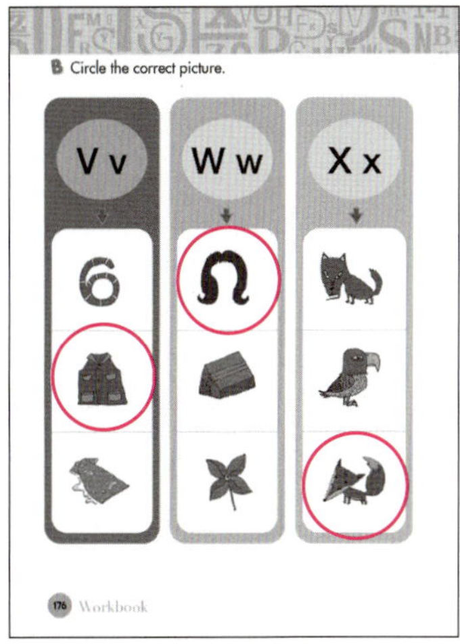

181p

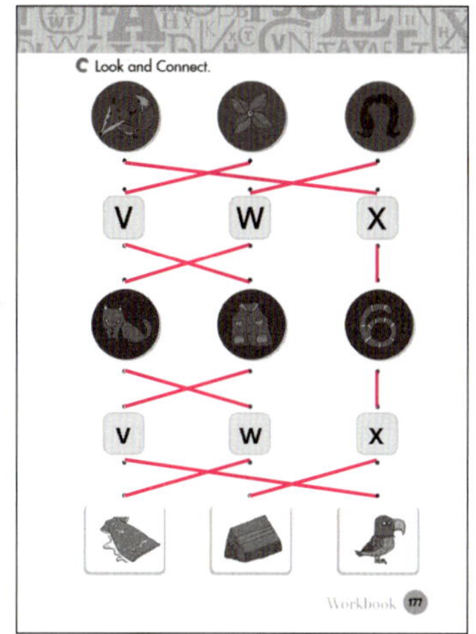

182p

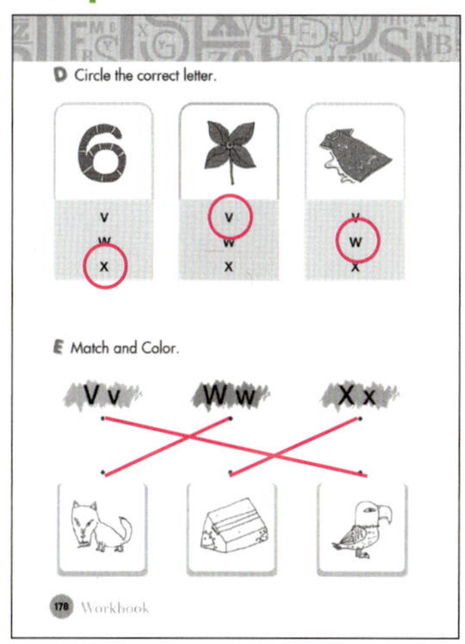

185p

186p

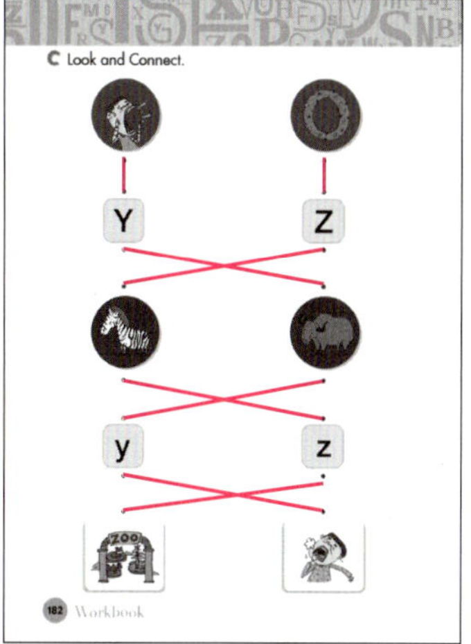

187p

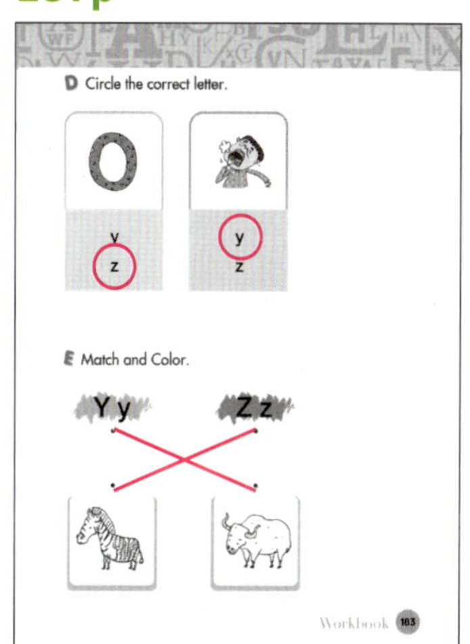

189p

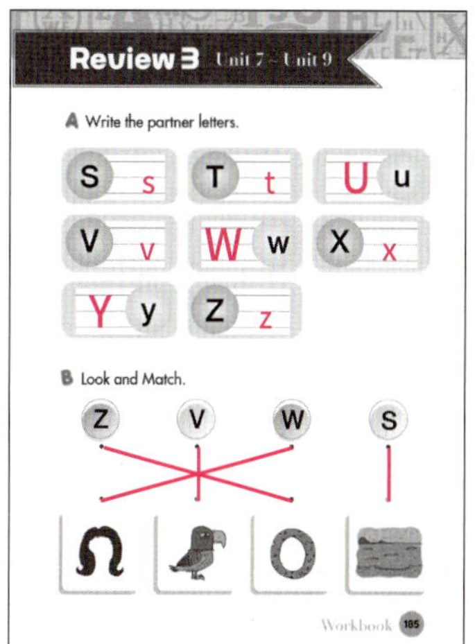

Answer Key

190p

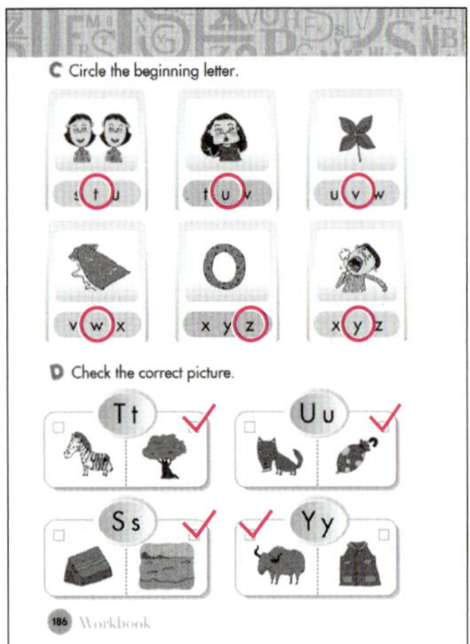

191p

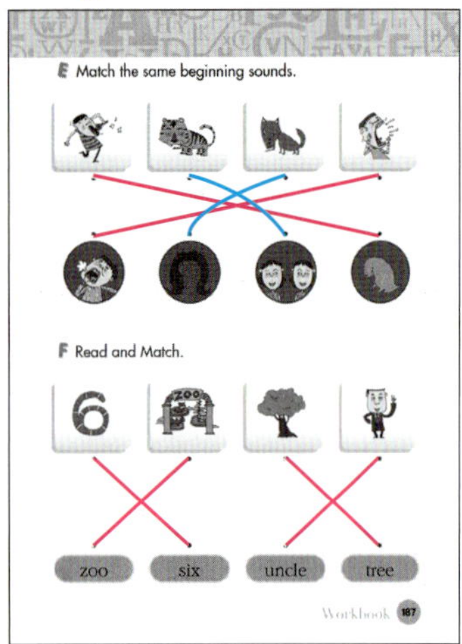

192p

193p

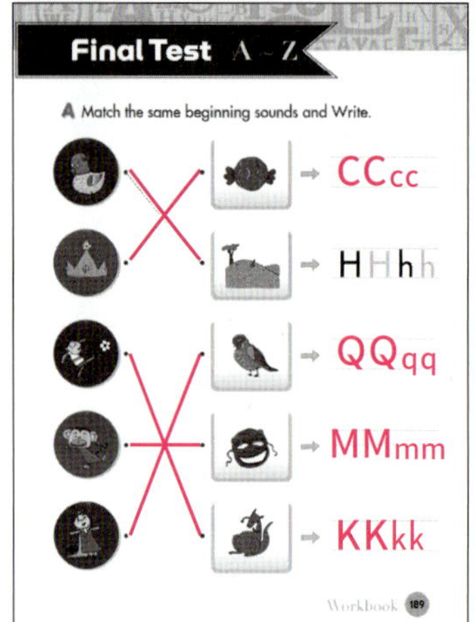

194p

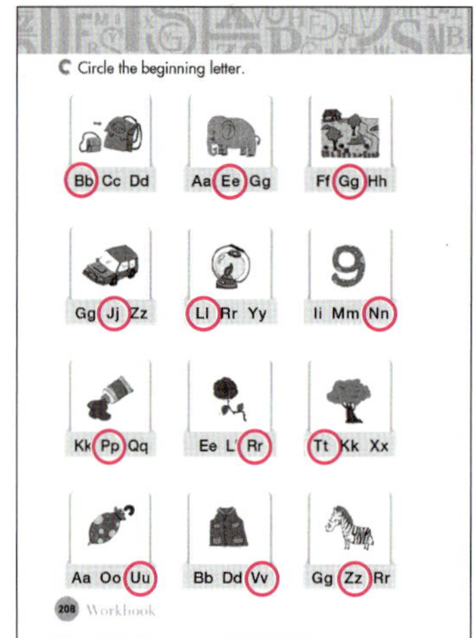

195p